# Nabokov's Deceptive World

# Nabokov's Deceptive World

*William Woodin Rowe*

New York: New York University Press
1971

## ACKNOWLEDGMENTS

*Thanks are due the following for their kind permission to use passages from the works indicated:*

From EUGENE ONEGIN: A NOVEL BY ALEKSANDER PUSHKIN, translated from the Russian, with a commentary by Vladimir Nabokov, Bollingen Series LXXII, Princeton University Press (copyright © 1964 by Bollingen Foundation, New York). Reprinted by permission of Princeton University Press.

From Vladimir Nabokov's LAUGHTER IN THE DARK. Copyright © 1938 by Vladimir Nabokov. Reprinted by permission of New Directions Publishing Corporation.

From Vladimir Nabokov's BEND SINISTER. Copyright © 1960 by George Weidenfeld & Nicolson Limited (London) for the British Commonwealth and Empire except Canada and by McGraw-Hill, Inc., for the United States and Canada. Reprinted by permission of the author, George Weidenfeld & Nicolson Limited, and McGraw-Hill, Inc.

From Vladimir Nabokov's SPEAK, MEMORY. Copyright © by George Weidenfeld & Nicolson Limited (London). Reprinted by permission of the author in the United States and Canada and by permission of George Weidenfeld & Nicolson Limited in the British Commonwealth and Empire except Canada.

From Vladimir Nabokov's DESPAIR. Copyright © 1966 by G. P. Putnam's Sons for the United States and Canada and by George Weidenfeld & Nicolson Limited (London) for the British Commonwealth and Empire except Canada. Reprinted by permission of the author, G. P. Putnam's Sons, and George Weidenfeld & Nicolson Limited.

From Vladimir Nabokov's KING, QUEEN, KNAVE. Copyright © 1968 by McGraw-Hill, Inc., for the United States and Canada and by George Weidenfeld & Nicolson Limited (London) for the British Commonwealth and Empire except Canada. Reprinted by permission of the author, McGraw-Hill, Inc., and George Weidenfeld & Nicolson Limited.

From Vladimir Nabokov's LOLITA. Copyright © 1959 by G. P. Putnam's Sons for the United States and Canada and by George Weidenfeld & Nicolson Limited (London) for the British Commonwealth and Empire except Canada. Reprinted by permission of the author, G. P. Putnam's Sons, and George Weidenfeld & Nicolson Limited.

From Vladimir Nabokov's ADA. Copyright © 1969 by McGraw-Hill, Inc. Reprinted by permission of the author and McGraw-Hill, Inc.

*Contents*

v

. . . Nabokov is the living master of English prose . . .

*Clarence Brown*

I reread my books rarely, and then only for the utilitarian purpose of controlling a translation or checking a new edition; but when I do go through them again, what pleases me most is the wayside murmur of this or that hidden theme.

*Vladimir Nabokov*

# Introduction

When Stanley Edgar Hyman published his opinion "It is about time we recognized that Vladimir Nabokov is a novelist of major importance"[1] in 1966, his words may still have been appropriate. Now they seem dated. Not only has *Lolita,* as Nabokov informed me in a recent interview, been translated into more than forty languages, John Leonard entitled his review of *Ada* (*The New York Times,* May 1, 1969) "The Nobel-est writer of them All."

Nabokov's world reflects the intricacies and manipulations of its creation. F. W. Dupee finds that he "has been able to perfect an English prose medium whose flexibility is adapted to the astonishing range, the endless contradictions, of his nature, of Nature itself."[2] In his autobiography *Speak, Memory,* Nabokov views nature and art as united through deception:

> I discovered in nature the nonutilitarian delights that I sought in art. Both were a form of magic, both were a game of intricate enchantment and deception.[3]

Similar sentiments recur constantly in his novels.[4]

The mechanisms involved in the creation of Nabokov's deceptive world have heretofore not been examined at book length. The present study aims to examine his deceptive art, an art that Alfred Appel, Jr. has termed "artifice or nothing."[5]

One essential feature of Nabokov's style perhaps requires at least brief preliminary discussion. He frequently spices the words of his narrators and characters with an unwitting clairvoyance which sometimes is evident even to the careful reader only in retrospect. Such ironic prophecies, or prophetic ironies, have never before been so systematically employed, although Nabokov hardly invented the effect. Shakespeare's Hamlet tells Horatio, early in the play, "We'll teach you to drink deep ere you depart," [6] obviously unaware that he will emphatically dissuade Horatio from emptying the poisoned cup in the final scene, where the latter has just been "taught to drink deep" by lavish example indeed. The second sentence of Gogol's "Nevsky Prospect" opens with the joyous, panegyric exclamation "What this street does not shine with . . ." and compares it to a beautiful girl.[7] Only in the famous ending of this story, when Satan lights the street lamps at night "just to show everything in an unreal aspect" and "when the entire town turns into thunder and gleaming light," [8] only then is the prophetic irony fully realized. (The effect is reinforced in the Russian by the similarity of "shine," *blestit,* to "gleaming light," *blesk.*)

Flaubert, whom Nabokov admires, has Homais rather ironically predict the success of Emma Bovary's beauty in Rouen. But the most biting ironic prophecies lead to a reverse result: poison for pleasure *(Hamlet),* evil gleam for innocent shine ("Nevsky Prospect"). Thus, Charles Bovary implies that Rouen might be good for Emma and stresses earlier that horseback riding is healthy. But compared to some of Nabokov's these last two prophetic ironies seem quite muted.

The more one reads Nabokov, the more each individual word seems a purposeful participant in the total, uniquely calculated world of his works. Details give rise to surprisingly fresh echoes and reflections elsewhere—from line to line, from book to book. Words and phrases seem faintly but undeniably to catch many others in the prism of their associations and connotations, almost as if Nabokov's entire *oeuvre* were planned from the very first. Thus the reader experiences a curiously timeless sensation of *déjà vu,* and Nabokov's world seems structured by a single, systematic, and complex creative mechanism.

This effect of uniquely interechoing *déjà vu* seems to derive from Nabokov's belief that

> ... imagination is a form of memory. ... In this sense, both memory and imagination are a negation of time.[9]

Nabokov's method of composition also seems pertinent:

> The pattern of the thing precedes the thing. I fill in the gaps of the crossword at any spot I happen to choose. These bits I write on index cards until the novel is done.[10]

> Since I always have at the very start a curiously clear picture of the entire novel before me or above me, I find cards especially convenient when not following the logical sequence of chapters but preparing instead this or that passage at any point of the novel and filling in the gaps in no special order.[11]

Such a method of composition seems ideally suited for establishing a refreshingly precarious balance between repetition and originality. It also of course facilitates Nabokovian ironic prophecies. And perhaps Humbert's phrase "trivial and fateful detail" [12] hints at the very essence of Nabokov's art.

But no solitary volume can suffice. It is hoped that this one will prove helpful; that even its strange appendices will serve as worksheets for further analysis. For it appears that Nabokov—partially by means of the mechanisms revealed below—will continue to flutter the pulses of his readers for some time. "He will continue to be read," Page Stegner has suggested,

> for the brilliance of his language and sharpness of his observation, for his impressionistic rendering of reality. One comes away from a Nabokov novel awed by many things, but chiefly by the dazzling display of verbal skill. . . .[13]

I am especially grateful for a National Endowment for the Humanities grant, obtained through New York University, which sustained the writing of this book. Many thanks go also to my wife Eleanor, whose incisive observations and occasional dissuasions proved invaluable. Following distant stars that glow only for him, the persevering critic of Nabokov sometimes fails to notice, upon his triumphant arrival, that someone has quietly tilted the sky.[14]

## Notes

1. Stanley Edgar Hyman, *Standards: A Chronicle of Books for Our Time* (New York, 1966), p. 188.
2. F. W. Dupee, *"The King of the Cats" and Other Remarks on Writers and Writing* (New York, 1965), p. 141.
3. Vladimir Nabokov, *Speak, Memory* (New York, 1966), p. 125.
4. Hermann asserts that "every work of art is a deception" [*Despair* (New York), 1966, p. 188]. Fyodor tells Zina: "The most enchanting things in nature and art are based on deception." (*The Gift*, New York, 1963, p. 409.) Of Axel Rex we are somewhat paradoxically told: "Perhaps the only real thing about him was his innate conviction that everything that had ever been created in the domain of art, science or sentiment, was only a more or less clever trick." [*Laughter in the Dark* (New York), 1961, p. 100.] And, in Nabokov's *Eugene Onegin* Commentary, one finds:

    > . . . true art is never simple, being always an elaborate, magical deception. . . .
    > Art is a magical deception, as all nature is magic and deception.

    [*Eugene Onegin* (New York), 1964, Vol. III, p. 498.]

    Nabokov also maintains, of *EO*, that "Pushkin's composition is first of all and above all a phenomenon of style." (I, 7) And he dubs Pushkin "a deceiver as all artists are." (I, 50) Both observations seem especially appropriate with regard to Nabokov and his own writing. We should note however that "artists" and "deceivers," thus combined, seem insidiously more synonymous than the statement in fact claims. But this is itself a deception, and highly typical of Nabokov.
    Recently questioned about the purpose of magic, sleight-of-hand, and other tricks in his fiction, Nabokov replied:

    > Deception is practiced even more beautifully by that other V.N., Visible Nature. . . . A grateful spectator is content to applaud the the grace with which the masked performer melts into Nature's background.

    [Vladimir Nabokov Talks About Nabokov," *Vogue* (December, 1969), p. 190.]

5. Alfred Appel, Jr., "Nabokov's Puppet Show," *The Single Voice*, Jerome Charyn, ed. (London, 1969), p. 78.

6. *Hamlet*, I, ii, 175.

7. N. V. Gogol, *Collected Works in Six Volumes* (Moscow, 1959), Vol. III, p. 7. Unless otherwise specified, all translations from the Russian are my own.

8. *Ibid.*, p. 43. Gogol can be seen to have constructed, with what in retrospect seems somewhat disturbing thoroughness, an invisible bridge between his initial innocent and final diabolical shinings. First, "shining" (*blestyashchim*) store windows appear in a sentence with a faintly ominous statement about heavy footsteps under which, "*it seems*, the very granite cracks. . . ." (p. 8; my italics) Then, of the ladies' handkerchiefs we are told: "*It seems* as if an entire sea of moths has suddenly risen up . . . in an agitated, shining [*blestyashcheyu*] cloud. . . ." (P. 10; my italics.) Finally, Satan's eerie lighting of the streetlamps is preceded by: "Oh, do not trust this Nevsky Prospect! . . .

All is deception. . . . all is not what *it seems!*"

[P. 42; my italics.]

9. "An Interview with Vladimir Nabokov" (Conducted by Alfred Appel, Jr.), *Nabokov: The Man and His Work*, L. S. Dembo, ed. (Madison, Wisconsin, 1967), p. 32.

10. Vladimir Nabokov, "The Art of Fiction," *The Paris Review*, No. 41, p. 102.

11. "An Interview with Vladimir Nabokov," p. 24.

12. Vladimir Nabokov, *Lolita* (New York, 1959), p. 102.

13. Page Stegner, *Escape into Aesthetics: The Art of Vladimir Nabokov* (New York, 1966), p. 44.

14. As Matthew Hodgart has phrased it, Nabokov's books abound in booby-traps that are not meant to kill or mutilate (Nabokov is not a sadist), but merely to blow the critic's pants off, leaving him standing in ludicrous half-nakedness, missing something." [Happy Families," *The New York Review* (May 22, 1969), p. 3.] But the general fairness of Nabokov's challenge tends to deprive this "merely" of its rightful ironic bite.

*Nabokov's Deceptive World*

*Part I*
*A Touch*
*of Russian*

# 1.

## *Negation*

Nabokov's ultimately startling use of negation can perhaps be related to a "positive" descriptive force in Russian that functions quite dramatically in the so-called "negative comparison" (*otritsatel'noe sravnenie*), a figure especially typical of old Russian folklore but occurring to this day in both poetry and prose.[1]

Essentially the device first denies one idea or image and then attempts to affirm a similar one. For example:

> Stormy winds have not sprung up,
> Uninvited guests have driven up.[2]

Despite their denial, the "stormy winds" perversely and vividly serve as a positive descriptive force. By virtue of first focusing upon a suggestively similar image, the negative comparison produces a final effect at once both fresh and familiar. The device owes part of its power to negative psychology and an element of briefly ensuing suspense. It can comprise a long enumeration of initially negated detail that slowly and somewhat paradoxically serves to clarify the final, cumulatively bright image. Consider only these four lines from Pushkin:

> A flock of ravens did not fly down
> Upon piles of moldering bones:

> At night, beyond the Volga, around fires,
> A band of fierce brigands gathered.

Among other unseen subtleties here the first, and stressed, syllable of "raven" in Russian is *vor* ("thief"), but the "positive" effect of this negation should be clear.

Similar effects may be found in Nabokov's Russian prose. In his short story "Ultima Thule" we are told that the "collective sleep" of a certain house

> . . . was abruptly—no, not disturbed, but shattered, splintered by sounds which remained unforgettable for those who heard them. . . . It was not the pig-like squeals of a tender coward hastily killed by villains in a ditch, and not the roaring of a wounded soldier, whom a brutal surgeon somehow liberates from his gigantic leg, they were worse, oh, worse. . . . I guess they resembled most of all the choking, almost triumphant cries of a woman in endlessly painful labor, but a woman with a masculine voice and with a giant in her womb.[3]

This passage utilizes descriptive forces similar to those of the negative comparison. Despite its denial, the word "disturbed" tends to prepare us for the intruding noises, just as the speciously negated "squeals" and "roaring" help to characterize the final "cries." Typically, the terminal, enduring effect is a carefully cumulative construct. Note also the relatively subtle touches that link the final image to what has been "denied": masculine— soldier; giant—gigantic; triumphant—liberated.[4]

*Speak, Memory* contains a close approximation of the negative comparison in English. Recalling "two sleighs slipping away" in the distance when he was a child, Nabokov writes:

> The vibration in my ears is no longer their receding bells, but only my blood singing.[5]

In an earlier and slightly different version ("Mademoiselle O") the form is even closer to its potentially Russian origin:

No, even the vibration in my ears is not their receding bells, but my own blood singing.[6]

The purely "Russian" form, of course, would read something like: "Their receding bells were not vibrating in my ears; my own blood was singing there." [7]

With ingenious modification, Nabokov often utilizes descriptive forces not unlike those at work in the negative comparison in his English novels. Consider Humbert Humbert, irrevocably repulsed and about to leave Lolita forever:

> Then I pulled out my automatic—I mean, this is the kind of a fool thing a reader might suppose I did. It never even occurred to me do it.[8]

Presumably it did occur to Humbert, just as it compellingly occurred to him to describe this murky urge. The implications are, however, that he viciously killed the temptation, whose ghost vividly lingers, not unlike the initial image in a negative comparison. Earlier on the same page, Humbert remarks:

> I was surprised (this is a rhetorical figure, I was not) that the sight of the old car in which she had ridden as a child and a nymphet, left her so very indifferent.

Our final impression is that Humbert was somewhat surprised, at least on one level. In fact, the power of this scene draws deeply upon the tension between Humbert's hopeful desperation and Lolita's "surprising" indifference. Thanks to incomplete negation, the initial, denied image typically, vividly lingers. This is especially so here because the words following Humbert's negation subtly and cumulatively suggest his potential surprise. Note also the psychologically very. double-edged phrase "in which she had ridden as a child." Humbert then adds—humorously or tragically, or both—"and a nymphet," and his moral ambivalence is transmitted to the reader through the uncomfortable juxtaposition of "child" and "nymphet."

Dining at The Enchanted Hunters, Lolita notices a man she describes as resembling Quilty, and Humbert tells us that "her sharp brown elbow" was

> not pointing, but visibly burning to point, at the lone diner in the loud checks, in the far corner of the room.[9]

Aided as usual by vivid detail, negation strangely promotes the final impression. In view of what is to occur, Humbert's "perceptiveness" has a faint flavor of Nabokovian irony.

Humbert reports John Farlow's offer "to help" after Charlotte's death:

> ". . . and you may sleep with Jean"—(he did not really add that but Jean supported his offer so passionately that it might be implied).[10]

Even though denied, the original image humorously returns—at least in Humbert's mind!—to a surprisingly viable state of affirmation.

Similarly, the narrator of *The Real Life of Sebastian Knight*, denied access to a hotel register in his long and frustrating search, writes:

> I turned on my heel and slammed the door after me,—at least, I tried to slam it,—it was one of those confounded pneumatic doors which resist."

Despite its playfulness, the image is especially vivid in its unrealized intention.

Such humor can be subtly muted by the reader's sympathy. When Luzhin (chess-playing hero of *The Defense*) is on the brink of insanity from the strain of intense protracted competition, he is described as

> . . . obtaining his first point by defeating an extremely te-

nacious Hungarian; the game, it is true, had been postponed after forty moves, but the continuation was perfectly clear to Luzhin.[12]

In *Lolita,* Humbert constantly describes a large part of the truth through denial. For instance:

> We are not sex fiends! We do not rape as good soldiers do. We are unhappy, mild, dog-eyed gentlemen . . . ready to give years and years of life for one chance to touch a nymphet.[13]

The form is quite unlike a negative comparison but the same forces function. "Ready to give years and years to touch" reaffirms much of the initial "sex-fiend" denial. The partial truth of the intervening words however serves to disguise the effect. Consider also: "I am not a criminal sexual psychopath taking indecent liberties with a child." [14] The mechanism behind this clever parade of partial truths is quite complex. Nevertheless, "taking indecent liberties with a child" (by virtue of whatever accuracy it has) tends to affirm the initially denied notion of "criminal sexual psychopath."

Nabokov's surprisingly "positive" negation can be extremely succinct. The denial can spring to life in a single word. When Lolita leaves for camp, having just kissed Humbert good-bye, we read: "The next instant I heard her—alive, *unraped*—clatter downstairs." [15] What physical reality loses, Humbert's mental one seems to gain. Though amazingly telescoped, the single word "unraped" seems to conjure up Humbert's initial urges, their denial, and the lingering reality of their imagined realization. The effect is similar to that of Smurov's *(The Eye)* statement (upon reading a letter that describes him as a "sexual lefty"): "I cleared my throat and with *untrembling* hands tidily folded the sheets." [16] True as "unraped" and "untrembling" may be, it is the inner struggles they evoke and depict that remain to haunt the reader. Consider also Hermann's description of himself, struggling desperately against total madness near the end of *Despair:* "Calmly, without cursing, I got up and. . . ." [17]

Or the device may take shape as a humorously protracted, self-belying elaboration of negated detail:

> I did not plan to marry poor Charlotte in order to eliminate her in some vulgar, gruesome and dangerous manner such as killing her by placing five bichloride-of-mercury tablets in her preprandial sherry or anything like that; but a delicately allied, pharmacopoeial thought did tinkle in my sonorous and clouded brain.[18]

This darkly humorous opening greatly resembles the first image of a negative comparison, strengthened in English by the word "but." Its morbidly belabored detail is multiplied by dual hints at much more ("such as . . . or anything like that"). Already the truth seems perversely close to what the words deny. And the suspiciously beside-the-point connotations of "vulgar, gruesome and dangerous" (plus the implications of this very word order!) also contribute to the effect. Nabokov soon justifies our anticipations:

> I saw myself administering a powerful sleeping potion to both mother and daughter so as to fondle the latter through the night with perfect impunity. The house was full of Charlotte's snore, while Lolita hardly breathed in her sleep, as still as a painted girl-child. "Mother, I swear Kenny never even *touched* me." "You either lie, Dolores Haze, or it was an incubus." No, I would not go that far.

The picture is now framed ("I did not . . . I would not . . .") by surprisingly ineffectual negation. Especially in a re-reading, much of the humor can be seen to derive from the initially denied but suspiciously precise words "placing" and "five."

Nabokov creates a similar effect early in the novel, as Humbert "reminds" the reader of a long list of sexually accomplished "children" he has lovingly culled from the pages of history. The list is interrupted near the top by some rather carefully calculated negation:

This is all very interesting, and I daresay you see me already frothing at the mouth in a fit; but no, I am not; I am just winking happy thoughts into a little tiddle cup.[19]

As usual, the negation seems weak almost in proportion to the force of its emphasis. Especially effective is the speciously proleptic admission to a hypothetical reader that these "happy thoughts" are "interesting," when they obviously *fascinate* Humbert. And the image of himself that he "grants" the reader seems filled with suspiciously plausible detail. The long historical list of youthful lovings finally closes with some "scientific" facts concerning "the bud-stage of breast development" and "the first appearance of pigmented pubic hair," whereupon Humbert remarks: "My little cup brims with tiddles." [20] But what of the word "just" in the passage above? The contrast it strained to imply (between "frothing" and "winking") tends humorously and abruptly to pale now that the (rather obviously frothing) tiddle cup returns. Indeed, the initial, negated image (as in a negative comparison) now seems surprisingly consistent with the finally established one.

Nabokovian negation occasionally describes by implication, by suggestion. "Don't do that," says Humbert to Charlotte while eloquently refusing to go to England with her. At last he concludes his reasons, and we learn that she is "clawing at" his trousers and suggesting they "make love rightaway." [21] Martha *(King, Queen, Knave)* similarly evokes a vivid picture of Franz's (completely undescribed) amorous advances:

He would let me know—no, no Franz, not now, after supper perhaps. I think he meant to be an example to his little wife, who otherwise might visit him—I said no—without warning in that little room with the couch he has at the back of his office.[22]

Franz's repulsed advances are subtly intensified by Dreyer's implied ones.[23]

Early in *Lolita* Humbert states that he adores her "so hor-
ribly." Immediately terming this "wrong," he replaces "horrible"
by "pathetic." He then goes on to conclude that the latter word
should "qualify" the former.[24] (The descriptive force persuades
much like a negative comparison.) Humbert describes his return
to Ramsdale:

> No dog barked. No gardener telephoned. No Miss Opposite
> sat on the vined porch. . . .[25]

Together, these denied details vividly re-evoke Humbert's previous
description of Charlotte's death and its aftermath.

*Laughter in the Dark* and *King, Queen, Knave* are rich in
evocative negations that emphasize the petty thoughts and desires
abounding in these two novels. Consider Dreyer's *not* buying
fruit for his train trip:

> . . . he did not put his head out of the window, did not
> beckon with a soft "psst" the young vendor in the white
> jacket.[26]

Negation promotes the very image that Dreyer, by inference,
struggles to deny his own desires. The Dreyers' party begins:

> Martha checked her hairdo and walked quickly—not to the
> front door but back to the door of the drawing room in order
> to make an elegant entrance from afar to meet her guests.[27]

Here the dash before the word "not" subtly forces the reader to
pause and change pace much as Martha no doubt did, when
almost blundering into unaffectness.

Early in *Laughter in the Dark* we see Margot preying upon
Albinus' pity for her past and, when comforted,

> . . . smiling through her tears, which was difficult, seeing
> there were no tears to smile through.[28]

But it was not so difficult, we easily infer, to prevent even her mediocre display from deceiving an eagerly compassionate Albinus. Margot's tears effectively linger. Axel Rex, whose swindling tendencies are by no means limited to love-making, is "negatively" exposed as follows:

> They could have given him a better room for his money (which, he thought, they might never see).[29]

By dint of negation the reader is maneuvered into envisioning a disappearance of money quite similar to the one implied.

In the Robinsons' *(Ada)* "badly insulated cabin" aboard the *Tobakoff*:

> . . . one could hear every word and whine of two children being put to bed by a silent seasick nurse, so late, so late— no, not children, but probably very young, very much disappointed honeymooners.[30]

The implied naïveté of "disappointed" tends faintly to reaffirm the original image of "children." And before she leaves the room, the hapless nurse seems to evoke both childishness and inhibitions. A similar humorous, haunting twist derives from a brief description of Van late in the novel: "At ninety, he still danced on his hands—in a recurrent dream." [31] The initial image, though abruptly abolished, instantly resurrects itself as Van's mental image, with which the reader involuntarily identifies his own. (Earlier, one watched Van's body; now one is suddenly in his mind.) The reader of course should have known better: Van had been unable to stand on his hands for years.

In Nabokov's short story "An Affair of Honor," the entire elaborately described "ending" is suddenly interrupted by: "Such things don't happen in real life" [32] and replaced by a much shorter, and sadder dénouement. The first ending lingers, however, like a vivid desperate daydream that really did take place in the hero's tortured mind.

Nabokov's use of protagonist narrators often affords him opportunities to control "reality" through negation. On the second page of *Despair* Hermann admits having already lied to the reader but purposely leaves the lie behind as a sample of one of his "essential traits": his "light-hearted, inspired lying." [33] *This* narrator is obviously never to be trusted without risk. Indeed, it often seems safer to take the opposite of what he says.

> And speaking of literature, there is not a thing about it that I do not know. It has always been quite a hobby of mine. As a child I composed verse and elaborate stories. I never stole peaches from the hothouse of the North Russian landowner whose steward my father was. I never buried cats alive. I never twisted the arms of playmates weaker than myself. . . .[34]

Axel Rex's childhood seems even more obviously to parody Smerdyakov's.[35]

Such mendacious narration conduces to dark humor throughout. After murdering Felix, Hermann reports that ". . . both bag and gun were discarded—no, I will not say what I did with them: be silent, Rhenish waters!" [36] Soon he abruptly remarks: "Oh, no, I have never feared dead bodies, just as broken, shattered playthings do not frighten me." [37]

When V. (the narrator of *The Real Life of Sebastian Knight*) has finally seen through Madame Lecerf's elaborate deception, he offers her a long, shattering explanation for his sudden departure, beginning: " 'It was very clever of you,' I said. . . ." [38] Then, as his little speech terminates, he remarks:

> No, I did not say a word of all this. I just bowed myself out of the garden.

We immediately suspect that Madame Lecerf is probably clever enough to deduce at least some of V.'s unsaid speech, but still it seems strange that he did not avenge himself on her more completely. The next sentence reads: "She will be sent a copy of this book and will understand."

Negation relentlessly serves as a positive descriptive force in Nabokov's *Invitation to a Beheading*. When Cincinnatus climbs up to see out of his prison window we see Rodion the jailor observing him from below:

> This attractive Russian countenance was turned upwards toward Cincinnatus, who stepped on it with his naked sole —that is, his double stepped on it, while Cincinnatus himself had already descended from the chair to the table.[39]

The action and especially its evoked motivation effectively linger. Such manifestations of the prisoner's double increase in frequency as the beheading approaches.[40]

Cincinnatus thinks he discerns in a drawing by little Emmie some hidden indications that she will help him escape. A long description of her sketch terminates abruptly in:

> No—this was only self-deception, nonsense. The child had doodled aimlessly. . . . Nonsense, let's not dwell on it any more. . . .[41]

Yet the detailed picture of his escape remains, as do the prisoner's hopes. And perhaps there even lingers a faint, hopeful suggestion that the "child"—of whom Cincinnatus seems almost inordinately fond—envisioned subconsciously that which he reads at such vivid length into her "innocent" little scribbles.

Evocative negation also describes Rodion, who

> . . . cried out and cringed, as people cry out and cringe whom not a bat but an ordinary house mouse inspires with revulsion and terror.[42]

"Bat" is "flying mouse" in Russian. Even here however the ordinary house mouse seems deceptively, inspiringly batlike. And a strange mixture of unpleasant associations remains about the jailor.

Nabokov has expressed great admiration for Gogol's eerie employment of the words "even" and "almost." [43] The phrase "no, not quite" in *Invitation to a Beheading* promotes a similar eerieness. In the three short passages below—two early in the novel, the last one late—the reader can trace a crescendo of atmospheric fright. The first two describe the ceiling light in Cincinnatus' cell; the third sets the stage for his execution.

> . . . the slightly concave ceiling, with a light (wire-enclosed) in its center—no, that is, not quite in the center: a flaw that agonizingly irritated the eye. . . .[44]

> . . . the light came on in business-like fashion in the center of the ceiling—no, not quite in the center, that was just it— an agonizing reminder.[45]

> In the center of the plaza—no, not quite in the center, that was precisely the dreadful part—rose the vermilion platform of the scaffold.[46]

In *Ada* Nabokov abruptly negates three large areas of narration that perversely linger as valuable insights into Van Veen's inner thoughts and emotions. The first is a painfully candid letter from Van to his father presuming his, Van's, death in an impending duel and admitting the seduction of Ada, "who was then twelve." [47] While the reader is still weighing the effect of this letter upon Demon, narration continues:

> He carefully reread his letter—and carefully tore it up. The note he finally placed in his coat pocket was much briefer.

The "real" note simply apologizes for being killed in a useless duel. But Van's confession about Ada ("That happiness has been the greatest event in my life, and I have no regrets") signally lingers in the reader's mind, even though the first letter can be deemed somewhat suspicious (it contains some unlikely lines about a "chap" who was "attempting oral intercourse" with a "washroom attendant, a toothless old cripple").

Similarly, Van abruptly "tears up a prepared speech" to "Mr. Rack" after more than fifty rather gripping lines presumably addressed to the latter.[48]

A further such unreal digression stems from Ada's writing to Van during their long separation:

> Would she write? Oh she did! Oh, every old thing turned out. . . .[49]

The ensuing narration, not without clues to its unreliability, vividly describes Ada's husband's dueling with Van, having called him out after learning "all" from Ada. Suddenly however the duel fades away into murky uncertainty:

> Van got his adversary plunk in the underbelly—a serious wound from which he recovered in due time, if at all (here the forking swims in the mist).

Such unreliable narration resides at the very heart of the novel, where the meanings of "time" and "reality" are deeply questioned. Next we read that

> Actually it was all much duller.
> So she did write as she had promised? Oh, yes, yes! In seventeen years he received from her. . . .

As in a negative comparison, the final image is surprisingly similar to its negated predecessor. Here, the telling method predicates a parallel-universe-like reality, wherein alternate possibilities happen "side by side"—or whatever spacial designation can suggest concurrent yet independent moments in Time.[50]

Nabokov's longest negated passages occur in *The Gift,* where a seven-page discussion (on the street between Fyodor and Koncheyev) that examines "the whole of Russian literature" terminates as follows:

"And what a pity no one has overheard the brilliant
colloquy that I would have liked so much to hold with you."
Never mind, it won't be wasted. In fact, I'm glad it
turned out this way. Whose business is it that actually we
parted at the very first corner, and that I have been reciting
a fictitious dialogue with myself as supplied by a self-teach-
ing handbook of literary inspiration? [51]

This rather whimsical twist raises some fundamental Nabokovian
questions: Was the colloquy wasted if it did not take place? Was
it any less real for being imagined? Was it not, in terms of opening
Fyodor's inner world to the reader, perhaps even more "real"?
And is not all art a paradoxical deception anyway—a deception
somehow more convincing when the effect is afterwards stressed
as unreal so that, as if by perverse contrast, it then seems surprisingly fresh and alive?

Fyodor's long-anticipated, moving, and dramatically presented
meeting with his father [52] is abruptly denied, yet its "reality"
vividly and indelibly lingers throughout the remainder of the
novel.

Other long, denied, but perversely lasting passages in *The
Gift* include Fyodor's detailed search for inspiration[53] and some
fun with alternate realities in Chernyshevski's "Life." [54] Nabokov
seems to be relentlessly examining the mechanism of a poet's
imagination. Later in the novel, Fyodor thinks a young German
on a bench resembles Koncheyev.

Imagination again—but what a pity: I had even thought
up a dead mother for him in order to trap truth. . . . Why can
a conversation with him never blossom out into reality,
break through to realization? Or is this a realization, and
nothing better is needed . . . since a real conversation would
be only disillusioning—with the stumps of stuttering, the
chaff of hemming and hawing, the debris of small words? [55]

Contrary to appearances, the above is quoted in full, the dots
suggesting omissions being a part of the text. But what surer
way to depict the process of thought? And what surer way to

vivify the imagined than to undermine the "real"? And what better insight into a poet's mind than through his imagination?

*Invitation to a Beheading* (the novel that Nabokov "esteems" over all his others [56]) ends with a dismantling of its scenery. The entire book may thus be seen as the first two components of a negative comparison—the novel proper being an initial image, the dismantling acting as its negation, and the reader's memory remaining to create the final effect.

Nabokov's constant narrational instrusions to admit, or even to insist that his effects are staged, artificial, or even false—can all be seen to enlist the reader's memory in similar reaffirmation.

Like many other Nabokovian devices and effects, his use of negation involves a superimposition of one "reality" upon another so that the final image, or impression, seems at once fresh and yet strangely familiar. As he has written in *Speak, Memory*:

> I like to fold my magic carpet, after use, in such a way as to superimpose one part of the pattern upon another. Let visitors trip.[57]

## Notes

1. In addition to the brief description below, please see Appendix A.
2. A. Potebnya, *Mysl' i yazyk* (Kharkov, 1913), p. 181.
3. Vladimir Nabokov, *Vesna v Fial'te i drugie rasskazy* (New York, 1956), p. 284.
4. After the above cries, a Dutchman runs out into

   > the garden, where the housekeeper already was, and eighteen paled maids (two in all, multiplied by the rush of running). (*Ibid.*, p. 285.)

   The amazing thing about this compact deception—even more compact in the Russian: only four words in the parentheses—is that its essence, the action, presumably no longer exists at the time of its apparent realization. But this possibly serves to speed it even further.
5. Vladimir Nabokov, *Speak, Memory* (New York, 1966), p. 100.
6. Vladimir Nabokov, *Nabokov's Dozen* (New York, 1958, p. 131.
7. Interestingly enough, the original Russian version is quite unlike a negative comparison; and thus Nabokov's English may be considered

more Russian in this instance than his Russian. See Vladimir Nabokov, *Drugie berega* (New York, 1954), p. 88.

8. Vladimir Nabokov, *Lolita* (New York, 1959), p. 255.

9. *Ibid.*, p. 112.

10. *Ibid.*, pp. 93-4.

11. Vladimir Nabokov, *The Real Life of Sebastian Knight* (Norfolk, Conn., 1959), p. 124.

12. Vladimir Nabokov, *The Defense* (New York, 1964), p. 117.

13. Nabokov, *Lolita*, p. 82.

14. *Ibid.*, p. 137.

15. *Ibid.*, p. 63. My italics.

16. Vladimir Nabokov, *The Eye* (New York, 1966), p. 91. My italics.

17. Vladimir Nabokov, *Despair* (New York, 1966), p. 210.

18. Nabokov, *Lolita*, p. 67.

19. *Ibid.*, p. 20.

20. *Ibid.*, p. 21.

21. *Ibid.*, p. 85.

22. Vladimir Nabokov, *King, Queen, Knave* (New York, 1968), p. 156.

23. See also Margot's vividly evocative statement to Albinus: "No, leave me alone tonight." (Vladimir Nabokov, *Laughter in the Dark*, New York, 1961, p. 76.)

24. Nabokov, *Lolita*, p. 59.

25. *Ibid.*, p. 263.

26. Nabokov, *King, Queen, Knave*, p. 8.

27. *Ibid.*, p. 141.

28. Nabokov, *Laughter in the Dark*, p. 56.

29. *Ibid.*, p. 78.

30. Vladimir Nabokov, *Ada* (New York, 1969), p. 492.

31. *Ibid.*, p. 571.

32. Vladimir Nabokov, *Nabokov's Quartet* (New York, 1966), p. 43.

33. Nabokov, *Despair*, p. 14. Compare: "Sorry, there really was no snake; it was just my fancy . . ." (p. 78) See also p. 41.

34. *Ibid.*, p. 55.

35. Not only did Rex also have a half-witted mother,

> As a child he had poured oil over live mice, set fire to them and watched them dart about for a few seconds like flaming meteors. And it is best not to inquire into the things he did to cats. (Nabokov, *Laughter in the Dark*, p. 78.)

Smerdyakov, it will be recalled, "loved very much to hang cats and bury them later, with ceremony." [F. M. Dostoevsky, *Collected Works* (Moscow, 1956-1958), Vol. IX, p. 158.]

Of course numerous passages in Nabokov seem teasingly to parody Dostoevsky (as distinguished from the relatively obvious Rascalnikov-Crime-and-Pun-Crime-and-Slime type). Compare Luzhin's viatic indecision, for example, with Mr. Golyadkin's—and Hermann's ecstatic lying with General Ivolgin's.

36. Nabokov, *Despair*, p. 184.

37. *Ibid.*, p. 193.

38. Nabokov, *The Real Life of Sebastian Knight*, p. 173.

39. Vladimir Nabokov, *Invitation to a Beheading* (New York, 1965), p. 29.

40. *Ibid.*, pp. 193, 198, 211.

41. *Ibid.*, p. 62.

42. *Ibid.*, p. 203.

43. See Vladimir Nabokov, *Nikolai Gogol* (New York, 1944), p. 142.

44. Nabokov, *Invitation to a Beheading*, p. 119.

45. *Ibid.*, p. 125.

46. *Ibid.*, p. 218.

47. Nabokov, *Ada*, pp. 308-9.

48. *Ibid.*, pp. 314-5. The same technique is employed in Nabokov's *Bend Sinister* (London, 1960):

> Yes, I am still jesting. We now come to the real thing.

(p. 107)

> No, it did not quite go on like that. In the first place Paduk was silent during most of the interview. What he did say . . .

( p. 131)

And, though somewhat muted, the technique persists:

> Which, of course, terminated the interview. Thus? Or perhaps in some other way? Did Krug really glance at the prepared speech? And if he did, was it really as silly as all that? He did; it was.

(p. 135)

As often happens in Nabokov, it is tempting to hear echoes elsewhere. Kinbote describes Emerald giving Gradus a lift:

> Did they talk in the car, these two characters, the man in green and the man in brown? Who can say? They did not.

[Vladimir Nabokov, *Pale Fire* (New York, 1966), p. 200.]

". . . this is reality," says Ada,

> . . . this cannot be taken away, can it? (it will, it was) . . ."

Nabokov, *Ada*, p. 153)

It is especially the haunting, cumulative effect of such subtly teasing parallels and mutual echoes that gives Nabokov's world its unique degree of tension between freshness and *déjà vu*.

49. Nabokov, *Ada*, p. 531.

50. Van's "suicide" suggests such alternate possibilities. No sooner has he "put the automatic to his head" and "pressed the comfortably concaved trigger," than we read:

> Nothing happened—or perhaps everything happened, and his destiny simply forked at that instant . . .

(*ibid.*, p. 45)

51. Vladimir Nabokov, *The Gift* (New York, 1963), p. 90.
52. *Ibid.,* pp. 396-9.
53. *Ibid.,* pp. 12-13.
54. See *ibid.,* pp. 15, 340.
55. *Ibid.,* p. 385.
56. "An Interview with Vladimir Nabokov" (Conducted by Alfred Appel, Jr.), *Nabokov: The Man and His Work,* L. S. Dembo, ed. (Madison, Wisconsin, 1967), p. 44.

    *Ada* of course had not yet appeared.

    In several ways, *Invitation to a Beheading* is strikingly similar to Yuri Olesha's *Envy.* Besides the basic parallel theme of creative imagination abused · by well organized philistinism, pertinent points of comparison include the use of geometric shapes, reflections and mirrors, muted homosexuality, and the "hostility" of things to people with creative ideas.

    Andrey Biely's *St. Petersburg* contains similar parallels.
57. Nabokov, *Speak, Memory,* p. 139.

# 2.

*Wordings
and Meanings*

Much critical attention has been accorded Nabokov's extensive parody of, and allusion to, Russian literature. Potential Russian influences, however, are considerably broader. Indeed, it can be said without much exaggeration that Nabokov—uniquely and justly deemed a master stylist in both languages—has adapted the English language to certain Russian modes of expression.

To begin with, it may be fruitful to investigate the surprisingly complex evocative effect of one specific type of Nabokovian allusion—the literal transplantation of wordings from various Russian authors. Pushkin of course begins *Eugene Onegin* with a highly evocative transplant *within* Russian literature, which Nabokov explains at great length.[1] By means of similar, but bi-literary transplants, Nabokov achieves a Russian emotional evocativeness in his English prose, even while the parodic character of this device sustains authorial detachment. A brief investigation of selected transplants from Pushkin, Apukhtin,[2] and Gogol may serve to demonstrate some of the effects of this mechanism.

Nabokov opens *Ada* with a twisting of the first sentence in Tolstoy's *Anna Karenina*. The following transpositions, worked smoothly and subtly into later dialogue, are perhaps better hidden, though no less evocative.

"*Tak ti zhenat* (so you are married)? Didn't know it. How long?"
"About two years."
"To whom?" [3]

From Nabokov's own translation of *Eugene Onegin:*

"So you are married! Didn't know before.
How long?" "About two years."
"To whom?" [4]

Especially the reader who knows the Russian original experiences a sudden, mind-wrenching combination of strange familiarity and deceptive freshness. Even more important, Onegin's (inferentially evoked) subsequent emotions set the stage for Van's bitter jealousy as Pitt proceeds to mention Ada's "numerous boy friends."

Similarly, Van informs Lucette: "I love you with a brother's love and maybe still more tenderly." [5] This is, word for word, Nabokov's translation of a statement by Onegin to Tatiana in Chapter Four of *EO*.[6] And the emotions evoked in Tatiana by Onegin's words seem most appropriate to Lucette's reaction here. Also in *Ada* the apparently innocent line, "Your uncle has most honest standards," [7] is a variation of Pushkin's opening line in *EO* "My uncle has most honest principles." And Onegin's desire for his uncle's death thus tinctures the rest of Van's sentence: "but I am going to demolish him soon."

Numerous suggestive details from the play in which Marina acts quite literally set the stage for Demon to possess her between two very *EO*-like scenes. Tatiana's romantic longings for Onegin are evoked by Marina's "flimsy and fetching nightgown," the "love letter" and "old nurse," and especially by "the artificial moonlight's blaze upon the lovelorn lady's bare arms and heaving breasts." [8]

Moreover, the tropical moonlight she had just bathed in, the penetrative sense of her own beauty, the ardent pulses

of the imagined maiden, and the gallant applause of an almost full house made her especially vulnerable to the tickle
of Demon's mustache.

We think immediately of Tatiana's "light chemise" that "has slid
down from her charming shoulder,"[9] her old nurse and love
letter, and especially of "the inspirative moon" that causes Tatiana's heart to range far away.[10] Note also that Nabokov's phrase
"the ardent pulses of the imagined maiden" refers equally well
both to Tatiana and to the Tatiana-like role played by Marina
immediately preceding her seduction behind the scenes. Finally,
"almost full house" adds a playfully ironic Nabokovian spice to
the affair.

Even within *Ada* this theatrical scene seems to prefigure the
also *EO*-like episode involving Van and "a pretty and proud young
nurse" called Tatiana ("a torturing angel in her own right")
deep in the novel.[11] Here, Van's amorous advances are repulsed
(like Onegin's) and she "much later" writes him "a charming
and melancholy letter" (like Tatiana's), but no affair ensues (also
as in *EO*). The order of events is reversed, but not the emotions
evoked.

Such potentially evocative phrases seem at times teasingly
unlikely. Do we hear echoes of Pushkin's punnish "our modest
author,"[12] for example, in Van's "the modest narrator"[13] and
the humorous sexual ambiguity of "modest Van"[14] almost four
hundred pages later?

In his Foreword to *Despair* Nabokov atypically reveals an
insertion of words from Russian literature.

The line and fragments of lines Hermann mutters in
Chapter Four come from Pushkin's short poem addressed to
his wife in the eighteen-thirties.[15]

Since such confessions are quite rare, the reader is continually
teased by evocative possibilities.

By means of transplanted wordings, Nabokov's Russian short
story "The Admiralty Needle" draws deeply upon the emotional

content and complexity of two poems by Apukhtin: "The Letter" (1882) and "The Answer to the Letter" (1885). In "The Letter," a woman confesses her readiness to rejoin a former lover who has abandoned her. "The Answer" abruptly rebukes the woman for making her letter public and yet summons her to "a sea, wide as passion, and a passion, wide as the sea." Both letters open with the line: "Upon seeing my handwriting, you will surely be surprised." Nabokov's story consists of a letter to the author of a novel which appears to be a distortion of the letter-writer's past love affair with a girl named Katya. (He is convinced that the author's masculine name, Sergey Solntsev, is a pseudonym.) The letter proceeds to rebuke "Katya" for exploiting the past, which includes Katya's fondness for poetry: "Upon seeing my handwriting, you will surely be surprised." [16] Here, the reader may recall that the letter-writer described the appearance of his own "handwriting" on the first page of Nabokov's story, fourteen pages earlier, where the name Apukhtin also casually appeared. The letter-writer hastens to add that he will restrain himself and not end his letter by inviting "Katya" to "a sea, wide as passion, and a passion, wide as the sea." Finally, he closes with the very faint but chilling possibility that "Sergey Solntsev" is not a pseudonym—thus tantalizingly undermining the emotions he has evoked through Apukhtin, which emotions linger as does his conviction that he has written to Katya after all. Obviously, the effect is somewhat weaker in translation, but the reader who recognizes the wording nevertheless experiences a unique feeling of overlapping realities.

In *The Defense* as Luzhin is said to be "going out of his mind not by the day but by the hour," Nabokov subtly constructs a giant backdrop of madness through casual reference to "yellow and red cornflowers," [17] which symbolic monsters hideously sprout in "The Madman," one of Apukhtin's very best, and worst, poems. Nabokov has "helped" the English reader by adding Apukhtin's name and making the quotation somewhat more obvious.[18] But even in translation the effect is quite powerful.

Evocative parallels in wording between Nabokov and Gogol range from obvious echoes to teasing similarities. In Gogol's

*Dead Souls* the following well-known passage depicts, in the window of the hotel where Chichikov first stops, a man

> . . . with a samovar of red copper and a face exactly as red as the samovar, so that from afar one could have thought that in the window were standing two samovars, if one samovar had not been with a black as pitch beard.[19]

The Russian word order has here been ruthlessly maintained in translation because it contributes to the humor. For example the words "two samovars" should immediately precede and thereby enhance the deception of "one samovar," which, in turn, should be deprived of the word "beard" as long as possible to sustain the deception.

Nabokov informs us in *King, Queen, Knave* that Mr. Piffke had

> . . . a profile that had prudently stopped halfway between man and teapot. . . .[20]

For a reader familiar with Gogol, the playful humor of this passage is considerably enriched. The word "prudently," moreover, can be read as an Aesopian authorial apology to those in the know. Most important, perhaps, just as Gogol's famous lover of boots loves on and on, in the endless night of some other dimension, so Gogol's samovar seems to make Piffke's profile keep straining to increase the humorous similarity between man and teapot.

In *The Gift*, we read:

> . . . Mme Chernyshevski, becoming for a moment—as usually happens—remarkably similar to her own (blue, gleaming) teapot. . . .[21]

Here the key words are, of course, "as usually happens," which serve to confirm a slightly humorous, but eerie pattern of repetition beneath the surface of "reality."

These evocative echoes seem reasonably obvious, but others are teasingly improbable. In Gogol's famous tale about the arguing Ivans, for instance, we read:

"No! . . . I cannot! . . . Give me another pen!" [22]

In *Lolita* Humbert Humbert exclaims:

". . . all New England for a lady-writer's pen!" [23]

In context, the Ivans' highly explosive friendship can be seen to help describe Humbert's friendship with Lo: the above sentence begins by his characterizing her as "Changeful, bad-tempered, cheerful. . . ."

Another such improbable parallel may be found between the well-known ending of the same Gogol story ("It is dreary in this world, ladies and gentlemen" [24]) and Lucette's pronouncement: "It's a dull life, Van." [25] (The Russian word *skuchno,* here rendered "dreary," is often translated "boring" or "dull.") Inferentially, the rollicking nonsense of Gogol's tale can be seen to color and characterize the various sexual pastimes and exploits that Lucette has just recounted. In context, both wordings similarly jolt the reader by showing the tears behind the laughter.

"Why does *phrasal tmesis* attract Nabokov?" Peter Lubin has asked.[26] "Could his use of the figure in English have something to do with the habit of loose word order in Russian?" (Most simply, the figure consists of inserting one or more words into a fixed phrase; Lubin's first example from Nabokov: "I'm all enchantment and ears.") "Isn't *phrasal tmesis* a syntactic equivalent of those 'specious lines of play' his books are filled with?" suggests Lubin. Tmesis, he cautiously concludes, "surprises":

The mind apprehends the terminal words which it expects to find juxtaposed, and then must accommodate the alien phonemes thrust between.[27]

"Must accommodate" is the key: when we read Nabokov we are often forced into vivifying creative participation.

Lubin terms the inserted portion of phrasal tmesis "a semantic petticoat" that is "slipped on between the naked noun and its clothing epithet." [28] In his example (from *Ada)* "safety gold pin," the petticoat is of course gold; "The resulting frou-frou," he suggests, "is quite satisfying." Developing the metaphor somewhat further, we may see phrasal tmesis as a veritable descriptive striptease, wherein the reader-spectator first sees clothing ("safety"), then petticoat ("gold"), then naked body ("pin"), which body has, however, been suggestively preshaped by the clothing already focused upon.

Such anticipatory effectiveness is a basic element of Nabokov's prose style.[29] Mariette *(Bend Sinister)* is described as follows:

> She had an irritating way of performing her household duties with nothing on to conceal her miserably young body . . .[30]

This improbably, but intriguingly begun sentence continues: "save a dim nightgown, the frayed hem of which hardly reached to her knees." Anyone experienced in translating from Russian into English knows the difficulty of fitting loose word order to stricter sequences. Note that if "nightgown" appears earlier, necessarily dragging along with it the "frayed hem" clause (". . . with nothing on save a dim nightgown, the frayed hem of which . . .")—the sentence must then end in an absurdity because "hardly reached to her knees" will be followed by "to conceal. . . ." Whether or not the flexibility of Russian could solve this problem, the point is that anyone thinking at least partially in Russian and writing in English is presumably apt to produce occasional initial effects similar to the above. Nabokov of course has a mastery of English that would preclude his ever leaving such a word order except, perhaps, where the resulting hold-off effect is both refreshingly successful and not overly awkward. Ronald Hingley has suggested that

> . . . Nabokov's English is justly described as masterly, per-

haps for the very reason that he puts twists on it such as would never occur to a native user.[31]

Note also, above, that as Nabokov's sentence is worded the initially naked Mariette, after she is clothed, leaves a final impression of nakedness—especially if we envision her frayed hem rising still higher (than "hardly reached to her knees") in the course of bending over to perform various household duties.

Not surprisingly *The Gift,* with its many long sentences, contains many such hold-off effects. For instance:

A "deep" matting swallowed without a trace the steps of the sentries pacing along the corridors.[32]

. . . a small child . . . was ironing the bench with a toy tank. . . .[33]

In both cases the Russian original contains the same word order.[34] The hold-off phrase "without a trace" however seems even more natural in the original, just as, conversely, the wording "was ironing with a toy tank the bench" would have been considerably smoother in Russian than in English.

The following example, also from *The Gift,* offers a hold-off effect that has been created by the English translation. Of young Chernyshevski, Fyodor writes:

. . . he was able to bend the silliest daydream into a logical horseshoe.[35]

The original Russian version begins with the (English) hold-off phrase: ". . . the silliest daydream he was able to bend into a logical horseshoe." [36]

After Franz breaks his glasses in *King, Queen, Knave,* Nabokov has inserted a brief but effective hold-off into his translation of the original: "Having negotiated the stairs, where an angel was singing as she polished the banisters, he . . ." [37] The words between the commas are new.[38]

Possible connections between the anticipatory hold-off effect and Nabokov's literary migration from Russian into English are of course complicated by the fact that he naturally favors the hold-off descriptive technique.[39]

It is no secret that Nabokov has both sought and received help with his English.[40] And little "mistakes" do seem occasionally to be made in Nabokov's English prose. Upon close scrutiny, however, nearly every one of these turns out to be a grammatically correct but faintly fresh, or "foreign," effect probably left on purpose, much as a painter might leave a tiny, unintended but mysteriously successful brush stroke. Moreover it should be emphasized that exceedingly few of Nabokov's narrators and characters have English as their first language; hence a foreign flavoring in their speech seems both natural and effective.[41] Often, such "foreign" wordings seem to derive directly from Russian modes of expression.

Word order is somewhat less flexible in English than in Russian, where adverbial modifiers frequently separate verbs from their direct objects:

... and proceeded to draw with incredible rapidity and very beautifully a racing car.[42]

... sat at a round table reading with an ironic expression on his face a Russian book.[43]

These two examples are taken, respectively, from *The Real Life of Sebastian Knight* and *Pale Fire*—both written originally in English.

In Russian, verbs meaning "to start" and "to finish" are normally followed by infinitives, not participles. Thus, when Humbert vividly plans to drown Charlotte while swimming ("... was finishing to tread his wife underfoot") his phrasing, though not really awkward, seems both strangely fresh and grimly deliberate. Where a novel has been translated from Russian into English, such constructions are of course more likely, for example, "commenced to swing" and "commenced to wash" (both from

*The Defense* [44]). Presumably, precise translation occasionally leads to similar unusual-infinitive effects: ". . . a magazine has offered me to edit its chess section. . . ." [45] But they also occur in originals; take *Lolita*:

> . . . I found a nice country road where to park in peace.[46]

> I really did not mind where to dwell provided I could . . .[47]

Or *Pale Fire*:

> I must renounce to give them verbatim in this commentary.[48]

In all three usages, the English infinitive translates somewhat more naturally into Russian.

It is tempting to sense a correspondence between the lack of definite and indefinite articles in Russian and Nabokov's fresh, vivid (and perhaps appreciative) usages thereof in English. These crystallize as "of the" and "of a" descriptive phrases.

> . . . she [Charlotte] of the noble nipple and massive thigh. . . .[49]

> . . . Lolita of the strident voice and the rich brown hair
> —of the bangs and the swirls at the sides and the curls at the back, and the sticky hot neck, and the vulgar vocabulary—"revolting," "super," "luscious," "goon," "drip"— . . .[50]

> . . . a pimply brute of a boy. . . .[51]

> . . . a small bulldog of a man. . . .[52]

There are numerous other instances.[53]

*Bend Sinister* and *Pale Fire* are relatively special situations wherein an imaginary language (often humorously) depends upon a knowledge of Russian. For instance Kinbote employs an astonishingly complex Russian-English word (wryly "translated") while describing Fleur, clad only in a short, sleeveless shirt: "The sight of her four bare limbs and three mousepits (Zemblan anatomy). . . ." [54] *Podmyshki* in Russian means "armpits." Moreover, *pod* means "under" and *mysh'* is "mouse." The total cumulative effect is ingenious and striking indeed. (Since this is Nabokov, we may note that when Van first notices Ada's pubic "floss" he recalls "the *mousy* charms of his first harlot." [55])

Also typically, in discussing methods of suicide Kinbote mentions jumping from a plane without a parachute: ". . . farewell, *shootka* (little chute)!" [56] *Shutka* is "joke" in Russian. The English spelling "shootka," however, retains the Russian pronunciation while conjuring up, bilingually, "little shoot"—most appropriate in the context of suicide.

In *Bend Sinister,* Krug's words *"Yer un dah"* are tersely "translated" in brackets as "stuff and nonsense." [57] The Russian word *erunda* (pronounced approximately "yerundah") means "nonsense."

In *Ada* and *Pnin,* Nabokov has created special worlds with a climate ideally suited to Russian linguistic influence. Without knowing Russian, one cannot understand completely even the first paragraph of *Ada,* wherein the word *Otrochestvo* ("Youth") is humorously confused with *Otechestvo* ("Fatherland") in allusion to "another Tolstoy work." [58] *Durak,* on the next page, means "fool," and so on. Much of the pleasure from reading *Ada* with a knowledge of Russian derives, however, from the fact that "translations," in parentheses, are so near and yet so far. In Chapter Two, for example, we read that Demon and Marina forgot "to dupe procreation,

> whereupon started the extremely *interesnoe polozhenie* ("interesting condition") without which, in fact, these anguished notes could not have been strung.[59]

In idiomatic usage, the Russian word *polozhenie* commonly signifies pregnancy. The "explanation" may occur without parentheses, as: "Gamlet, a half-Russian village. . . ." [60] Shakespeare's

*Hamlet*—like most English names beginning with "h"— is usually rendered in Russian *"Gamlet,"* rather than by the phonetically closer *"Khamlet."* Or, the "translation" or "explanation" may be absent entirely, as in the name "Bob Bean." [61] (*Bob* means "bean" in Russian.) Coined words also depend on Russian. Van refers to the six hundred and thirteen times he has been unfaithful to Ada as "obmanipulations (sham, insignificant strokings by unremembered cold hands)." [62] *Obman* in Russian means "deception."

To the reader's amusement, Pnin can often be heard thinking in Russian:

". . . there exist other troubles. It blows from the floor, and it blows from the walls—" [63]

"I do not want, John. You know I do not understand what is advertisement and what is not advertisement." [64]

"No, no," said Pnin, "I do not wish an egg or, for example, a torpedo. I want a simple football ball. Round!" [65]

The reader who knows no Russian may not fully savor these literal translations, but he can probably sense their delicious authenticity.

Some of Pnin's unwitting jokes seem more dependent upon a knowledge of Russian. For instance, Pnin declares he has "resolved not to use alcohol any more." [66] In spite of its humor in English, the infinitive "to use" *(upotreblyat')* is quite natural in Russian in such a construction.

The Russian language has a flexibility that is readily conducive to the coining of new words from old roots. From Pnin's name alone, Nabokov ingeniously produces, in English, Pninian, Pninizing, Pningrad and anti-Pninist.[67]

Nabokov is generally fond of coining new words and many of his inventions seem to reflect a fresh insight into English. Besides mousepits, he has devised such forms as: hobnailnobbing, nowanights, daymares, mauvemail, waltwhitmanesque, rosewise, stillicide, funnelform, nymphage, and ganch.[68]

Nabokov's English prose infrequently reveals apparent reflections of Russian words for which it is virtually impossible to find a natural English "equivalent." *Koe-kak,* for example, surfaces in English as "anyhow" (meaning "haphazardly").[69] Two other such Russian words are *sizyj* and *sivyj,* both of which signify slightly differing shades of gray. *Sizyj,* often used to describe pigeons or doves, evokes a grayish sheen with a faint bluish tinge. *Sivyj,* used typically to describe a gelding or someone's graying, silvering hair, also can suggest a smoky, or slightly bluish gray. Nabokov devises and very frequently employs similar shades of gray in his English prose. In *Lolita* alone:

pearl-gray [dress]
gauze-gray [room]
pale-gray [eyes]
dove-gray [cloud]
clouded-glass gray [eyes]
dream-gray [gaze]
grave gray [eyes]
pearl-gray [clothes] [70]

Also in *Lolita,* the following colors of cars seem especially suggestive of *sizyj* and *sivyj*:

Horizon Blue
Surf Gray
Dream Blue
Crest Blue
Shell Gray
Thistle Gray
French Gray
Dominion Blue [71]

In *Pnin,* the shadow of a tree seems to change color in appropriate response to a shift of narrational focus from turf to winter sky:

A skimpy squirrel dashed over a patch of sun-lit snow, where a tree trunk's shadow, olive-green on the turf, became grayish blue for a stretch, while the tree itself, with a brisk, scrabbly sound, ascended, naked, into the sky, where the pigeons swept by for a third and last time.[72]

The pigeons had just been described as "soaring gray, flapping white, and then gray again." Now, much as an ocean surface reflects the color of the sky, the "grayish blue" shadow here seems to reflect a pigeon-gray *(sizyj? sivyj?)* Russian sky above. Note also how the squirrel invisibly climbs the tree as focus moves upward.

Such theorizing is somewhat complicated by the fact that Nabokov greatly favors such "color-combination modifiers" anyway—at least fifty-seven in *Lolita,* fourteen each in *Pnin* and *Pale Fire,* twelve in *Despair,* and so on. Combinations with gray, however, seem favored most; of the twelve in *Despair,* three are dove-grey, two are mouse-grey. And Nabokov's Uncle Ruka is described as wearing a "dove-gray, mouse-gray or silver-gray summer suit." [73] Nabokov uses both spellings of "gray/grey," but phonetically it may be significant that "the long *a* of the English alphabet" has for him "the tint of weathered wood" and *r* suggests "a sooty rag being ripped." [74]

Generally Nabokov's color-combination modifiers reflect the resourcefulness and range of his agile imagination. Below is a short selection of the more unusual ones. Note that the word preceding the color sometimes has little or no connection whatsoever with the color itself, yet the final, modified noun crystallizes the cumulative image quite effectively:

*Lolita*

rubber-red [lips]
neon-blue [cottage]
coffin-black [volume]
the great rosegray [never-to-be-had]
watered-milk-white [arms]
gooseflesh white [arms] [75]

*Pale Fire*

blood-orange [sun]
blood-black [nothingness]
chalk-blue [berries]
kelp-brown [nets]
background gray [thought] [76]

*Speak, Memory*

the snow-blue, blue-windowed (the curtains are not yet drawn) [past][77]

*The Real Life of Sebastian Knight*

white-and-cinder-grey [trunk of a felled tree]
bug-brown [couch] [78]

*Pnin*

candy pink [cheeks]
a pathologically purplish [car] [79]

In a *two-page* short story by John Updike, who has not un-proudly avowed the influence of Nabokov, one finds "a baby-pink dean," "a dove-gray booklet," and "nicotine-orange fingers." [80]

Nabokov's ironic use of certain individual words may be seen to evince a faint influence both of Gogol and of a fresh insight into the English language. Russian of course was not Gogol's first language, and it seems quite natural that he was quick to notice the humorous potential of combinations such as:

In this same village there often appeared a person, or, *better,* a devil in human form.[81]

It is exceedingly difficult to animate these cold-blooded young
ladies or make them laugh; for this, one needs a great art or,
*better,* no art of any kind at all. . . . In high society one encounters them very seldom or *better,* never.[82]

Although the Russian word *luchshe* ("better") is more frequently
employed in this sense of "rather" or "more exactly," Nabokov
has nevertheless created similar effects in English:

. . . present day bards, owing to *better* opportunities of aging,
look like gorillas or vultures.[83]

. . . he visited us in Paris but twice,—*better* say once, for the
second time was when he came over for my mother's funeral.[84]

. . . and when she once tried searching his pockets, he gave
her such a rap on the knuckles that she decided to do it
*better* next time. . . .[85]

More often and more obviously, Nabokov employs the word
"good" with similar ironic effect:

Let me dally a little, he is as *good* as destroyed.[86]

Without his glasses he was as *good* as blind . . .[87]

One respectable burgher, who suddenly, for no *good* reason,
had dismembered a neighbor's child . . .[88]

Elsewhere I have suggested that such effects in both Nabokov
and Gogol may be termed perception-expanding reversals.[89] Pertinent mechanisms can be seen to range from abruptly ironic
usages of individual words to long, complex digressions wherein
narrational focus subtly and hauntingly returns to the point of
departure.

Prefixes and suffixes play a vital role in the formation of
Russian words. Nabokov's English often displays similar and

surprisingly natural manipulations. His favorite suffix is -let, and among prefixes, a-, be-, fore-, and re- most often occur. Resulting effects vary from a faint flavoring of older English to a heavy seasoning of wordplay. Below are a list of examples from Lolita alone:

aflame
a-jitter
afloat
a-jangle
a-whirr
ablaze [twice]
aglow [90]

bespectacled [twice]
bepearled
blood-bespattered
bepimpled
bemazed [91]

foreglimpsed
forehanging
foreglimpse [92]

townlet [twice]
playlet
chainlet [93]

re-fork
re-slammed
re-shouted [twice]
re-entered
recrossed
re-passed
repacked [94]

I pressed the bell button, it vibrated through my whole system. *Personne. Je resonne. Repersonne.* From what depth this re-nonsense? [95]

> A guardedly ironic silence answered my bell. . . . I tried the
> knocker. Re-nobody.[96]

The *a-* words tend to favor effects of heat or feverishness ("ablaze"
twice). They also tend to catch a state of movement or action.
*Be-* generally describes a surface covering; *fore-* and *-let* seem
obvious. *Re-* is surely the most playful in effect. And in the two
key dramatic passages above (the first precedes Humbert's last
meeting with Lolita; the second, his killing of Quilty), it seems to
provide a comic relief that by contrast somewhat paradoxically
serves to intensify the reader's rising suspense.

Generally, the most often repeated such forms in Nabokov's
English prose are *aflame, bespectacled, beribboned,* and *cloudlet.*
Some of the more unusual include:

> with . . . all the masks of the mind a-miming
> the swallows a-flying, and cloudlets a-high [97]

berimed
bewigged
besweatered
beslobber
bespit
befooled
beslushed
bejeweling [98]

forehear
foreshore
foretime
forefeels [99]

re-tuxedoed
re-grin
re-paning a broken window
re-offended
rechew and rebelch
re-vibrations [100]

paper baglet
faunlet
heartlet
tearlet
whorelet
nipplet
wartlet
beardlet
burbly flowlets
landaulet to Radugalet [101]

The last seven *-let* selections are all from *Ada,* which is especially rich in forms with the *-let* suffix.

Less frequently, Nabokov uses *pre-* and *-ette:*

presuicidal [102]

pedagoguette
colleenette [103]

And he occasionally uses standard forms in a metaphorical manner:

a brooklet of time [104]

Or with fresh meanings:

goblet [as a small gob]
recall [to call again] [105]

And even punnishly:

old letters *resent* being unfolded [106]

Roots in Russian words contribute far more obviously to meaning than do roots in English. Nabokov constantly combines

English words containing similarities between the letters and/or sounds of the root. The result is often a subtly alien and unexpected interplay of sense: "appre*hen*sive hen," "super*gal*actic gals," "*hands*ome hands," and so on.[107] The reader senses that unknown forces are at work behind the scenery, that each surface meaning obscures another one, both related and yet alien. Sound often seems calculated to develop sense more completely, as in "a vestige of vestibule," "our common hour."[108] Some of the effects are triple:

> . . . seascapes, escapes, capes . . .[109]

> . . . from the mast, from the past, and its castle tower . . .[110]

Others teasingly interplay between Russian and English:

> . . . if I bore you [*dokoochayou*] . . .[111]

> . . . hyperborean forest . . .[112]

*"Bor"* in Russian means a "coniferous forest."[113]

But Nabokov tends especially to favor effects that stress the ironic difference in meaning between surprisingly similar words. Hermann, in *Despair,* slyly asks:

> What is this jest in majesty? This ass in passion? How do God and Devil combine to form a live dog?[114]

Hermann also confesses that he enjoys making words "look self-conscious and foolish,"[115] but one suspects that Nabokov's preoccupation springs more from a fresh insight into English and a fondness for the strangely powerful effects often produced. Disparate meanings, speciously wed, subtly promote the reader's creative participation. Encountering ". . . there was not an earthly soul around, heeled or wheeled,"[116] for example, the reader must sift out meaning from sound, thereby partially contributing his own detail. Note also the unsettling Gogolian redundancy "earthly," which subtly furthers the evocative tension between meaning and printed appearance. Consider also Martha's *(King, Queen, Knave)* ". . . trying to dispell her *ill*ness by *will* power . . ." [117] wherein a similar tension [118] contributes to the struggle described.

Besides evocative words-within-words, Nabokov produces combinations of complementary words with an alteration of only one or two letters. In his *EO* Commentary, for example, he combines "matter" with "manner" no less than seven times.[119] Typical also are: "One man sinks, another drinks" [120] and ". . . as a Frenchman I preferred the grape to the grain." [121]

But such effects are particularly striking when they combine near opposites. In the *EO* Commentary, Nabokov digresses to mention that an 1837 misprint transformed "delight" into "poison" in Russian *(otradoy, otravoy)*; in his own Russian writing, the word *mirazh* ("mirage") is said to "turn simply into" *triazh* ("tyranny").[122] In *Lolita*, "friend" appears unsettlingly alongside "fiend," [123] and the reader is reminded of Nabokov's statement that Gogol's style

> . . . gives one of the sensation of something ludicrous and at the same time stellar, lurking constantly around the corner —and one likes to recall that the difference between the comic side of things and their cosmic side, depends upon one sibilant.[124]

The full impact of this passage however may only be experienced by reading from a greatly different, but strangely similar, part of Nabokov's world. In *The Gift*, we find the following signal juxtaposition:

> Only a few years earlier the smell of Gogol's Petrushka had been explained away by the fact that everything existing was rational. . . . There is always a danger, however, that one letter will fall out of the cosmic. . . .[125]

This verbal interplay is subtly strengthened by a haunting echo of wordings from book to book, and the phrase "always a danger" seems almost doubly ominous. Both Petrushka and "the cosmic," moreover, evoke inter-echoing suggestions of Gogol, who is of course but one of exceedingly many Russian literary and linguistic influences in Nabokov's world.

George Steiner has stated that

> We need really detailed study of the quality and degree of pressure which Russian puts on Nabokov's Anglo-American.[126]

The suggestions presented above are both tentative and limited, but hopefully they will lead to further investigation.

## *Notes*

1. See Vladimir Nabokov, *Eugene Onegin* (New York, 1964), vol. II, pp. 29-31.
2. A. N. Apukhtin (1841-93), a minor Russian poet of the late nineteenth century, whose knife-blade emotions and curious conceits are blemished by excessive sentimentalism.
3. Vladimir Nabokov, *Ada* (New York, 1969), p. 454.
4. Nabokov, *Eugene Onegin*, Vol. I, p. 300.
5. Nabokov, *Ada*, p. 481.
6. Nabokov, *Eugene Onegin*, Vol. I, p. 189.
7. Nabokov, *Ada*, p. 317.
8. *Ibid.*, p. 11.
9. Nabokov, *Eugene Onegin*, Vol. I, p. 172.
10. *Ibid.*, p. 163.
11. Nabokov, *Ada*, p. 312.
12. Nabokov, *Eugene Onegin*, Vol. I, p. 326.
13. Nabokov, *Ada*, p. 19.
14. *Ibid.*, p. 411.
15. Vladimir Nabokov, *Despair* (New York, 1966), p. 9.
16. Vladimir Nabokov, *Vesna v Fial'te i drugie rasskazy* (New York, 1956), p. 231. See also A. N. Apukhtin, *Stikhotvoreniya* (Leningrad, 1961), pp. 189, 221.
17. Vladimir Nabokov, *The Defense* (New York, 1964), p. 128. See also Apukhtin, pp. 239-40.
18. Vladimir Nabokov, *Zashchita Luzhina* (Paris, 1930), p. 140.
    Nabokov mentions Apukhtin elsewhere; see *The Gift* (New York,

1963), p. 169 and (presumably) *ibid.*, pp. 169-170; *Speak, Memory* (New York, 1966), p. 225.

19. N. V. Gogol, *Collected Works in Six Volumes* (Moscow, 1959), vol. V, p. 8.
20. Vladimir Nabokov, *King, Queen, Knave* (New York, 1968), p. 77.
21. Nabokov, *The Gift*, p. 43.
22. Gogol, *Collected Works*, Vol. II, p. 240.
23. Vladimir Nabokov, *Lolita* (New York, 1959), p. 47.
24. Gogol, *Collected Works*, Vol. II, p. 245.
25. Nabokov, *Ada*, p. 464.
26. Peter Lubin, "Kickshaws and Motley," *TriQuarterly* (Winter, 1970), p. 195.

     Recently speaking of Peter Lubin with the present writer, Nabokov said: "He is a genius." And of the parodic interview in Lubin's article Nabokov intriguingly offered: "He's more like me than I am."
27. *Ibid.*, p. 196.
28. *Ibid.*, pp. 194-5.
29. It may also help to explain Nabokov's obvious fondness for Pushkin's enjambments in *EO*, as well as the frequent and pleasing enjambments in his own poetry.
30. Vladimir Nabokov, *Bend Sinister* (London, 1960), p. 141.
31. Ronald Hingley, "An Aggressively Private Person," *The New York Times Book Review* (January 15, 1967), p. 16.
32. Nabokov, *The Gift*, p. 305.
33. *Ibid.*, p. 354.
34. See Vladimir Nabokov, *Dar* (New York, 1952), pp. 303, 352.
35. Nabokov, *The Gift*, p. 249.
36. Nabokov, *Dar*, p. 249. (The Russian word *duga* usually means "arc" or "bow," not "horseshoe.")
37. Nabokov, *King, Queen, Knave*, p. 23.
38. See Vladimir Nabokov, *Korol', dama, valet* (New York, 1969), p. 26.
39. In *The Gift* Zina looks up at the evening sky:

     "Look," she said. "What a beauty!"
     A brooch with three rubies was gliding over the dark velvet so high that not even the hum of the engine was audible.

     (p. 407)

     The effect is especially deceptive because of a "garnet brooch" mentioned twelve pages earlier. Similarly, "ram horns" gradually become Fyodor's first bicycle (p. 36).
     Typical also is Nabokov's description in the *EO* Commentary of Sheremetev, "shot through the breast" in a duel: "In his ire and agony, the poor fellow flapped and plunged all over the snow like a large fish." (Vol. II, p. 89) Only with the last word "fish" do the two verbs spring to fully justified life. The words "all over the snow" (and even "like a large") allow the total image to mellow, and ripen.
     In *The Gift* we read of "the opinions held by Skabichevski and Mihailovski about Chekhov—opinions that, like a fuse lit at the time,

have now blown these critics to bits." (p. 227) The printed pause here aptly parallels the pictured one.

In "That in Aleppo Once" we read of "that blinding blast which is caused by merely picking up a small doll from the floor of a carefully abandoned house: the soldier involved hears nothing. . . ." (*Nabokov's Dozen*, New York, 1958, p. 104) Mostly in retrospect, the word "carefully" does much of the detonating.

In *Speak, Memory* Nabokov follows the discussion of his colored hearing by:

> The confessions of a synesthete must sound tedious and pretentious to those who are protected from such leakings and drafts by more solid walls than mine are.

(p. 35)

"Protected" prepares for (but also patiently needs) "solid walls" to complete the image.

Finally, an entire sentence may be used to sustain the hold-off effect:

> It will be noted that the stanza of fourteen lines invented by Pushkin for *EO* is technically a French odic stanza from the waist up (the first seven lines being rhymed similarly in both). It may be said that the *EO* stanza is half ode and half sonnet. We might term it the mermaid stanza.

(*Eugene Onegin*, vol. II, p. 449)

The tmesis-like construction, of course, consists of "from the waist up" and "mermaid."

40. See Gleb Struve's "Letter to the Editor," *Novoye Russkoye Slovo* (December 12, 1967) and Lucie Léon Noel's remarks in *TriQuarterly* (Winter, 1970), pp. 214-5.

41. Even when Lolita, whose language usually epitomizes the sloppy American teenager's jargon of her time, asks "Does not he look exactly, but exactly, like . . . ?" (p. 112), her uncharacteristic grammatical stiffness may be deemed Europeanized in the alembic of Humbert's memory.

42. Vladimir Nabokov, *The Real Life of Sebastian Knight* (Norfolk, Conn., 1959), p. 144.

43. Vladimir Nabokov, *Pale Fire* (New York, 1966), p. 199.

44. Nabokov, *The Defense*, pp. 38, 248.

45. *Ibid.*, p. 127.

46. Nabokov, *Lolita*, p. 129.

47. *Ibid.*, p. 161.

48. Nabokov, *Pale Fire*, p. 134.

49. Nabokov, *Lolita*, p. 72.

50. *Ibid.*, p. 62.

51. *Ibid.*, p. 106.

52. *Ibid.*, p. 79.

53. *Of the:*

> Grandma of the beaming wrinkles
>
> Viola, of the blackheads and the bouncing bust
>
> Nathalie of the lovely bare shoulders and long earrings
>
> he of the embroidered blouse and bald head
>
> naughty Margaret Ann of the mint-flavored mouth and nimble fingers
>
> (*Nikolai Gogol,* New York, 1944, p. 66; *Lolita,* p. 51; *Nabokov's Dozen,* pp. 104, 126; *Speak, Memory,* p. 250, respectively.)

*Of a:*

> that gloomy giant of a man
>
> an old hole of a room
>
> a dusty hole of a room
>
> a mountebank of a man
>
> a genial giant of a man
>
> a great bully of a man
>
> (*Lolita,* p. 175; *Pale Fire,* pp. 87, 97; *Despair,* p. 114; *Pnin,* New York, 1965, p. 50; *Nabokov's Dozen,* p. 86, respectively)

54. Nabokov, *Pale Fire,* p. 80.
55. Nabokov, *Ada,* pp. 59-60. My italics.
56. Nabokov, *Pale Fire,* p. 158.
57. Nabokov, *Bend Sinister,* p. 80.
58. Nabokov, *Ada,* p. 3.
59. *Ibid.,* p. 15.
60. *Ibid.,* p. 35.
61. *Ibid.,* p. 25.
62. *Ibid.,* p. 195.
63. Nabokov, *Pnin,* p. 36.
64. *Ibid.,* p. 60.
65. *Ibid.,* p. 99.
66. *Ibid.,* p. 36.
67. See *ibid.,* pp. 15, 35, 63, 141, respectively. See also repetitions, pp. 39, 41, 66, 69, 149, 187.
68. *Nabokov's Dozen,* p. 151; *Speak, Memory,* p. 109; *Lolita,* pp. 231, 67; *Bend Sinister,* pp. 85, 120; *Invitation to a Beheading* (New York, 1965), p. 193; *Eugene Onegin,* vol. II, p. 68; *Lolita,* p. 62; *Ada,* p. 464, respectively.
69. Nabokov, *The Defense,* p. 58 (*Zashchita Luzhina,* p. 69). For similar uses of "anyhow" in Nabokov's English, see *Pnin,* p. 123 and *The Gift,* pp. 175, 180.

Speaking of this problem, Nabokov recalled the difficulty of translating *kak-nibud'* ("somehow") in *EO*. See Nabokov's translation, Vol. I, p. 97 and his note, Vol. II, p. 45.

70. Nabokov, *Lolita*, pp. 22, 23, 43, 140, 186, 234, 260, 264, respectively.
71. All, *ibid.*, p. 208.
72. Nabokov, *Pnin*, p. 73.
73. Nabokov, *Speak, Memory*, p. 69.
74. *Ibid.*, p. 34. Hard *g* is not given.
75. Nabokov, *Lolita*, pp. 63, 202, 239, 241, 246, 253, respectively.
76. Nabokov, *Pale Fire*, pp. 25, 41, 53, 105, 194, respectively.
77. Nabokov, *Speak, Memory*, p. 38.
78. Nabokov *The Real Life of Sebastian Knight*, pp. 139, 143.
79. Nabokov, *Pnin*, pp. 26, 35.
80. See *The New Yorker* (November 15, 1969), pp. 57-8.
81. Gogol, *Collected Works*, Vol. I, p. 44. My italics.
82. *Ibid.*, vol. III, pp. 31-2. My italics.
83. Nabokov, *Pale Fire*, p. 16. My italics.
84. Nabokov, *The Real Life of Sebastian Knight*, p. 28. My italics.
85. Vladimir Nabokov, *Laughter in the Dark* (New York, 1961), p. 21. My italics.
86. Nabokov, *Lolita*, p. 257. My italics.
87. Nabokov, *King, Queen, Knave*, p. 22. My italics.
88. *Ibid.*, p. 206. My italics.
89. See "Gogolesque Perception-Expanding Reversals in Nabokov," *Slavic Review* (March, 1971).
90. Nabokov, *Lolita*, pp. 58, 102, 120, 128, 135, 153, 189, 264.
91. *Ibid.*, pp. 54, 173, 148, 159, 173, 225.
92. *Ibid.*, pp. 115, 127, 241.
93. *Ibid.*, pp. 105, 163, 183, 190.
94. *Ibid.*, pp. 15, 63, 69, 250, 120, 141, 142, 247.
95. *Ibid.*, p. 245.
96. *Ibid.*, p. 267.
97. *Pnin*, p. 12; *Invitation to a Beheading*, p. 40. See also "asquat," *Ada*, p. 267.
98. "Berimed"—*Speak, Memory*, pp. 105, 235; *Pale Fire*, p. 12. The rest —*Speak, Memory*, p. 236; *The Defense*, p. 201; *Despair*, pp. 114, 152; *The Gift*, pp. 198, 314; *Nabokov's Dozen*, p. 140.
99. *Pnin*, p. 47; *Nabokov's Dozen*, p. 44; *Pale Fire*, pp. 26, 158.
100. *King, Queen, Knave*, p. 219; *Pnin*, p. 160; *Pale Fire*, pp. 178, 198; *The Gift*, p. 409; *Invitation to a Beheading*, p. 13.
101. *King, Queen, Knave*, p. 258; *Pale Fire*, p. 89; *Despair*, p. 191; *The Defense*, p. 162; "whorelet"—*Ada*, pp. 33, 168, 542; the rest—*Ada*, pp. 118, 513, 73, 24, 150.
102. Vladimir Nabokov, *The Eye* (New York, 1966), p. 18.
103. *Invitation to a Beheading*, p. 96; *Ada*, p. 216.
104. Nabokov, *Speak, Memory*, p. 292.
105. *Ada*, p. 52; Vladimir Nabokov, *The Waltz Invention* (New York, 1966), p. 58.
106. Nabokov, *The Real Life of Sebastian Knight*, p. 42. My italics.

107. *The Defense*, p. 98; *Nabokov's Dozen*, pp. 147, 148, respectively.
108. Nabokov, *Pale Fire*, pp. 12, 30.
109. Nabokov, *Pnin*, p. 92.
110. Nabokov, *Speak, Memory*, p. 50.
111. Nabokov, *The Real Life of Sebastian Knight*, p. 186.
112. Nabokov, *Eugene Onegin*, vol. II, p. 470.
113. See *ibid.*, p. 518.
114. Nabokov, *Despair*, p. 56. Chuckling at this ridiculous bit of fun, the reader is likely to miss the far larger joke that Hermann immediately makes:

> For several years I was haunted by a very singular and very nasty dream: I dreamed I was standing in the middle of a long passage with a door at the bottom, and passionately wanting, but not daring to go and open it, and then deciding at last to go, which I accordingly did . . .

Racing on to complete the "very nasty" dream, the reader may easily miss its sustained metaphor of Hermann as a piece of (his own!) excrement. The "long passage" with its "door at the bottom" is humorously supported by two potential puns on "to go." Most important, the wordplay process that Hermann has just revealed ("this ass in passion") offers three signal punnish clues: *na*sty, *pa*ssage, *pa*ssionately.

115. *Ibid.*, p. 56.
116. Nabokov, *Pnin*, p. 113.
117. Nabokov, *King, Queen, Knave*, p. 139. My italics.
118. Such evocative tension is anyway a basic ingredient of Nabokov's style. Normally incompatible words often combine to produce a vividly evocative effect. "Truffles," for example, are termed "delicious fungi" (*Eugene Onegin*, Vol. II, p. 73) and "fiddling" becomes "unlubricated music" (*The Gift*, p. 321). Typical also are "lyrics that tiptoed," "tortured his hat," "a masterpiece of erosion," "glorious bugs," "lyrical spasm" and "an orgy of corrections" (*Pnin*, p. 180; *King, Queen, Knave*, p. 54; *Pale Fire*, p. 103; *Nabokov's Dozen*, pp. 81, 27; *The Real Life of Sebastian Knight*, p. 83, respectively).
The effect frequently involves an unexpected personification, but this can be quite subtle.

> I remember Sebastian as a boy, six years my senior, *gloriously messing* about with water-colours in the *homely aura* of a *stately kersosene* lamp . . .
>
> (*The Real Life of Sebastian Knight*, p. 16, my italics)

The three italicized combinations all produce an unusual tension inviting the reader's vivid, reconciliatory participation.
Such tension often derives from the evocative irony of lightly oxymoronic combinations: "heavenly woe," "wonderful obsession," "lugubriously comfortable," "blissfully condemned" (*Despair*, pp. 36, 39; *The Real Life of Sebastian Knight*, pp. 180, 46).

In its most extreme form, the device becomes almost brazenly oxymoronic. Humbert speaks, for instance, of his "timid claws," his "vulgar darling," and describes himself (about to kill Quilty) as "lucidly insane, crazily calm." (*Lolita*, pp. 53, 109, 268) At times, such oxymoronic combinations seem quite ingeniously justified. Kinbote, noticing a car wheel spinning on a slippery winter driveway, speaks of its "concave inferno of ice." (*Pale Fire*, p. 12) More subtly, Humbert mentions "the hot thunder" of Lolita's "whisper." (*Lolita*, p. 122) (Here, one must associate "thunder" with "cold" for the full effect.)

119. Nabokov, *Eugene Onegin*, Vol. I, pp. 18, 34, 35: Vol. II, pp. 45, 277; Vol. III, pp. 33, 322.
120. Nabokov, *Tne Waltz Invention*, p. 19.
121. Vladimir Nabokov, *Nabokov's Quartet* (New York, 1966), p. 87.
122. Nabokov, *Eugene Onegin*, Vol. II, p. 393; *Vesna v Fial'te i drugie rasskazy*, p. 186, respectively.
123. Nabokov, *Lolita*, p. 245. See also "preferred ladies to laddies" (*Pale Fire*, p. 76).
124. Nabokov, *Nikolai Gogol*, p. 142.
125. Nabokov, *The Gift*, p. 274.
126. George Steiner, "Extraterritorial," *TriQuarterly* (Winter, 1970), p. 125.

*Part II*
*Nabokov as*
*Stage Manager*

# 3.

## Sound Effects

As Carl Proffer has noted, sound instrumentation is a foremost element of Nabokov's prose. "Even where an epithet appears to have been chosen because of its sound," he suggests, "it usually turns out that phonetic deftness is complemented by novelty of expression and precision of meaning." [1] One can go still further: orchestration constantly, actively and systematically contributes to meaning in Nabokov's works.

Generally, the technique functions not unlike background music that subtly intensifies an effect on stage or screen. Consider the following typical but relatively simple instance from *Laughter in the Dark*. Albinus has just become blind:

> Remembered scenes peopled the picture gallery of his mind: Margot in a figured apron drawing aside a *pur*ple *cur*tain (how he *year*ned for its dingy color now!) . . .[2]

Despite the light irony of "dingy," a repeated "ur" sound here vividly interacts to evoke Albinus' emotions. The purple curtain subtly intensifies his yearning, just as this yearning returns phonetically to seek its goal. Notice also that even the "no longer seeable" curtain disappears ("drawing aside"), which only serves, indirectly, to focus in upon the object his eyes miss most: Margot.

Nabokov seems to use assonance less frequently than alliteration (as Proffer has found [3]); but when sound contributes actively to meaning, assonance almost invariably does much of the work, as in the example above. During a summer abroad, the boy Luzhin *(The Defense)* learns of plans to return "to Russia—and the ghost of sch*oo*l, which his father dared not mention, again l*oo*med into vi*ew*." [4] Clearly enough, the *oo* assonance here vivifies the hauntingly unmentioned ghost. In the next sentence, we read that Luzhin's mother had returned to Russia earlier.

> She said she was *insanely* homesick for the Russian countryside, and that protracted "ins*a*nely" with such a pl*a*intive, *a*ching middle syllable was practically the sole inton*a*tion of hers that Luzhin ret*ai*ned in his memory.

The italics of the first *insanely* are Nabokov's. A sustained long *a* sound phonetically demonstrates and describes the intonation that Luzhin retains in his memory. In the Russian original, a repeated *oo* sound functions instructively throughout all of the above.[5]

In his *EO* Commentary Nabokov explains the expression "between wolf and dog" as "a familiar Gallicism . . . meaning dusk—a time of day when it is already too dark for the shepherd to distinguish his dog from a wolf."

> An evolutionist sense has also been read into the locution; namely, the reference to the blending of day with night in terms of an intermediary stage between two closely allied species of animals.[6]

But this very blending finds instructive demonstration in the phonetic merging of "evolutionist" and "locution." Such contributions to meaning by sound are vital to Nabokov's style. He himself speaks elsewhere in the Commentary of an *"ornamental support"* [7] which may be provided by alliteration, but Kinbote comes closer to explaining the Nabokovian effect in his note to the following lines of "Pale Fire."

> I was the shadow of the waxwing slain
> By feigned remoteness in the windowpane.[8]

The assonance between "feigned" and the rhyme, Kinbote claims, "gives the ear a kind of languorous pleasure as would the echo of some half-remembered sorrowful song *whose strain is more meaningful than its words.*" [9]

Late in *The Gift*, the poet Fyodor is falling asleep:

> His mind sank lower into a hell of alligator alliterations, into infernal cooperatives of words.[10]

The eight alliterative *l*'s seem obvious. The sound that promotes meaning here, however, features assonance as well: inf*e*rnal co-op*e*ratives of w*o*rds (and, more faintly, low*e*r . . . alligator allit-*e*rations).

Earlier in the novel, St. Petersburg ladies watching *Othello* are described as "devoured at that moment with envy for Desdemona." [11] Alliterative *d*'s, *m*'s, *n*'s, and *v*'s all contribute to the effect here, but stressed long *o*'s (moment, Desdemona) more signally emphasize and even phonetically illustrate the ladies' "envious" awe.

Similarly, a "crew of waiters" in *Ada* are described as "keeping a multiple eye on the tray that had flown back to Van with a load of gold change and bank notes." [12] By virtue of the long *o* assonance, we can easily picture the rounded wonder of the waiters' eyes and perhaps even their mouths.

When Humbert first sees Lolita, he is inspiringly reminded of his former Riviera love-mate: ". . . I saw again her lovely indrawn abdomen where my s*ou*thb*ou*nd m*ou*th had briefly paused. . . ." [13] Despite Humbert's "pause," his triple assonance vividly directs the reader's eyes. This sound, moreover, adds a not-inappropriate howl of delight to Humbert's find; he is, after all, the same hound that will soon "try to pick up a nymphet's scent" on Charlotte's body, "baying" nightly "through the undergrowth of dark decaying forests." [14] In the Russian version of

*Lolita,* "mouth" is slightly altered to "lips" *(guby),* which in context has a vivifying phonetic affinity with south *(yug).*[15]

In Chapter One of *Despair,* Hermann conveys a change in scenery partially by means of sound.

> Then all of a sudden the row of houses broke, disclosing a vast stretch of land that at first glance seemed to me most rural and alluring.[16]

The abrupt change in repeated assonances strikingly parallels a precisely concomitant alteration of terrain. And even the echoing long *o* in *most* can be seen to presage, by means of its phonetic incongruity, Hermann's disenchantment: the "splendor" of the land, we read, "proved to be a deception." Note also the suggestive phonetic interplay between "rural" and "alluring."

In *Bend Sinister* Nabokov derives a rather unique phonetic effect from the abrupt connotative alteration of the very same sound.

> . . . a young typist was poring over the contents of some documents, and so absorbed was she in deciphering them, and so noiselessly had the *ministr* entered, that she emitted a wild shriek when he snorted behind her back.[17]

With surprising success, the *or* sound loudly, abruptly invades and replaces the typist's quiet concentration.

*Speak, Memory* contains an unusual sentence (even for Nabokov) wherein a printed effect visually parallels [18] an also phonetically enhanced description. Nabokov has just visited the aging and almost totally deaf "Mademoiselle."

> At one spot a long light dimly diluted the darkness and transformed the mist into a visible drizzle.[19]

Al host of *d*'s and *l*'s almost visibly invades the word *mist,* transforming its printed letters into "visible drizzle" while retaining, however, the key familiar core of short *i* assonance. At this moment, Nabokov saw a clumsily struggling old swan and, although he "soon forgot that dismal night" (note the evocative echo in *dismal*), he connected "that night, that compound image" with Mademoiselle's death "a couple of years later." [20]

One rather unique and highly patterned type of sound arrangement used by Nabokov deserves special attention. Noting "the play of inner assonances that is so striking in *EO* and other poems by Pushkin," Nabokov pauses to offer two similar examples in English verse. The first is from Dryden:

> When *vapours* to their swimming brains ad*v*ance,
> And *double tapers* on the *table dance*

"Table" combines the first syllable of "tapers" and the second of "double"; "vapours" rhymes with "tapers"; and the initial consonants of these two words are repeated in the terminal rhyme, "advance-dance." [21]

Developing Nabokov's initial observation, we may designate the first component in the composite by 1, the second by 2, and the composite itself by 3. Thus, 2-1-3 denotes the pattern "*double tapers . . . table*," wherein ble = 2; ta = 1; table = 3.

The second example (from Wordsworth, and not followed by comment) fits a similar formula, as Nabokov's italics clearly indicate:

> . . . and, with a store
> Of indist*inguish*able sympathies,
> M*ing*ling most earnest *wish*es for the day . . .

Here, the pattern is 3-1-2. The advantage of such a construction is that one word or set of letters can join two apparently quite different ones, thus forming a triple phonetic link with no more than one repetition of any individual part. Sense is systematically, but subtly reinforced by sound.

Nabokov makes wide use, including many variations, of this

1-2-3 "Pushkin-like" [22] phonetic pattern. For example, describing images perceived just prior to falling asleep, he writes: "I am *pestered* by *roguish profiles. . . ."* [23] The pattern (1-2-3) is direct and simple, but surprisingly effective. By dint of phonetic affinity, the "profiles" seem pervasively "roguish," and they hauntingly "pester." And yet, because of its subtle structuring the entire effect acts quite unobtrusively.

Nabokov employs all of the six possible basic 1-2-3 combinations, but the pattern 2-1-3 seems to predominate:

g*ive* a *sh*am *shive*r [24]

a *li*ttle a*b*ode *of bli*ss [25]

t*ur*ned, and with a *s*light *lur*ch [26]

In the third example, he gains a supplementary effect from the two *t*'s that introduce 2 and connect 1 and 3. Similarly, in yet another 2-1-3 pattern "*fat pink Piff*ke," [27] the two "*k*"s subtly help make Piffke slightly pinker.

The letter *l* seems most often to participate in such supplementary effects. In the (3-1-2) example below, all three pattern parts are attended by an *l:*

the French window with its *f*uddled *f*ly between m*u*slin and pane [28]

And, when *l*'s are part of the basic pattern, supplementary *l*'s seem especially effective:

cut *gl*ass *gl*istened m*y*stically [29]

In this 1-3-2 pattern, the *l*'s in *mystically* tend to keep the glass glistening a fraction longer.

It should perhaps be stressed that the effectiveness of the specialized patterns discussed here derives from sound, not from

spelling. Thus, in the simple 1-2-3 phrase (with supplementary
*l*'s and *n*'s) "*p*ale flannel *p*ants," [30] the *a* of *p*ale is merely a
visual felicity. Conversely, in the 1-3-2 pattern "*r*ich *r*osy foam," [31]
the diphthong *oa* does serve phonetically to combine with the *r*
of *r*ich in closely approximating the *r*o of rosy. A more dramatic
example is "*s*ilently *sl*itted her  *eye*s," [32] where the *i* of slitted
is not akin to the one in *silently*, yet the *eye* in *eyes*, of course, is.
The pattern here (with supplementary *t*'s and a key *s*) is 3-1-2,
except that the *l* (*sl*) is split, in 3, to surround 2: *sil*.

Such "splits" may introduce one or more letters alien to
the components themselves:

cheap *s*weet *s*cent [33]

The *h*yper*b*ole is as *o*ld as the *h*ills [34]

In the first instance *w* separates; in the second, *yperb*. Note also
the typical *l*'s enhancing the second example.

Such splits may also be combined with a rearrangement of
letters so as almost to defy classification, such as

*ta*pe*r*ed to a *st*ra*n*ge sen*s*ation [35]

One subpattern, however, emerges quite clearly: an "overlap"
in parts 1 and 2. In the combination "*fl*ippantly *fl*at *l*ittle," [36] for
example, the letter *l* overlaps in 1 and 2 (*fl*, *li*) in producing 3
(*fli*). Similarly in "*sp*arkle-*sp*la*s*hed *p*latform" [37] the letter *p*
overlaps in 1 and 2 (*sp*, *p*la) in producing 3 (*spla*). Consider also
the faintly humorous

*Posh*kin, who when talking to people said "I *p*ot" for "I put"
and "*cosh*ion" for "cushion" . . . .[38]

The letter *o* overlaps in 1 and 2. By emphasizing both spelling
and sound, this instance subtly insinuates a humorous doom in
Poshkin's very name: his mispronunciations seem wryly inevitable.

In a more elaborate variation, Nabokov repeats one or more of the three phonetic parts for added effect.

r*un* a*mu*ck there in a*m*orous *m*adness [39]

The full pattern is 2-3-1-1, with supplementary *r*'s and the further combination *am-ma,* both halves of which drift off softly into terminal suggestive sibilance. Consider also

a *f*laccid, *f*atalistic, good-n*a*tured and *v*ague appeal to probability [40]

This 1-3-2-2 pattern is strengthened, in sound and meaning, by the suggestive phonetic similarity of *appeal* to *probability.* Finally, consider:

his *eye*s bri*mm*ed with the *diam*ond light of *m*adness [41]

Here, the pattern 1-2-3-2-1 forms a supporting phonetic crescendo just as the eyes flash their brightest.

It should be noted that this phonetic [42] patterning, especially in its more basic forms, often occurs in Nabokov's English [43] prose. Returning to the first passage discussed in this chapter (wherein sound enhances meaning: "purple curtain," "yearned"), we find a typical 2-3-1 effect in its opening words: "Remembered s*c*enes *p*eopled the *p*icture gallery of his mind. . . ."

Generally, assonance seems to predominate in those effects wherein sound contributes most to meaning. Alliteration is the armor—assonance, the inner life. And nowhere, perhaps, does Nabokov show more control or greater craftsmanship than in his meaningful manipulation of sound, including a great many variations of the 1-2-3 phonetic patterning described above.

## *Notes*

1. Carl R. Proffer, *Keys To Lolita* (Bloomington, Indiana, 1968), p. 82.
2. Vladimir Nabokov, *Laughter in the Dark* (New York, 1961), p. 140. My italics.

3. Proffer, p. 86.
4. Vladimir Nabokov, *The Defense* (New York, 1964), pp. 69-70. My italics.
5. Vladimir Nabokov, *Zashchita Luzhina* (Paris, 1930), p. 81. The key words are: *upomyanut', vernulas', bezumno toskuet, russkoj, zudyashchim.*
6. Vladimir Nabokov, *Eugene Onegin* (New York, 1964), Vol. II, pp. 484-5.
7. *Ibid.,* Vol. III, p. 534. My italics.
8. Vladimir Nabokov, *Pale Fire* (New York, 1966), p. 26.
9. *Ibid.,* p. 98. My italics.
10. Vladimir Nabokov, *The Gift* (New York, 1963), p. 395.
11. *Ibid.,* p. 117.
12. Vladimir Nabokov, *Ada* (New York, 1969), p. 413. My italics.
13. Vladimir Nabokov, *Lolita* (New York, 1959), p. 39. My italics.
14. *Ibid.,* p. 72.
15. Vladimir Nabokov, *Lolita* [in Russian] (New York, 1967), p. 29.
16. Vladimir Nabokov, *Despair* (New York, 1966), p. 16. My italics.
17. Vladimir Nabokov, *Bend Sinister* (London, 1960), pp. 125-6. My italics except for *"ministr."*
18. When the repetition of a group of letters contributes to meaning, the effect may be deemed both visual and phonetic: ". . . this slightly marred the marvel . . ." or ". . . as if in constant confirmation of. . . ." (*Despair*, p. 19; *Laughter in the Dark*, p. 14)
19. Vladimir Nabokov, *Speak, Memory* (New York, 1966), p. 116.
20. *Ibid.,* p. 117.
21. Nabokov, *Eugene Onegin,* Vol. III, p. 150.
22. Bryusov apparently noticed the effect in Pushkin but did not divide it into (its 2-1-3) components: "Eë zdorov'e *p*ervyj *p'ët.*" (Valerij Bryusov, *Moj Pushkin,* Moscow, 1929, p. 252) The next line ends "*p*eredaët."

    Discussing Gogol, Bely noticed but also did not patternize (as 3-2-1): "Step' kras*neet, s*i*neet, *gorit tsvetami" (Andrej Belyj, *Lug zelënyj,* New York, 1967, p. 119).

    A lovely variation may be found in *EO,* I, 20, 4:

    I, vzvi*v*shis', zana*v*es *s*humit.

In Nabokov's translation:

    and, soaring up, the curtain swishes.

23. Nabokov, *Speak, Memory,* p. 34. My italics.
24. Vladimir Nabokov, *The Eye* (New York, 1966), p. 7. My italics.
25. Vladimir Nabokov, *King, Queen, Knave* (New York, 1968), p. 11. My italics.
26. *Ibid.,* p. 3. My italics.
27. *Ibid.,* p. 233. My italics.
28. Vladimir Nabokov, *The Real Life of Sebastian Knight* (Norfolk, Conn., 1959), p. 9. My italics.

29. Nabokov, *The Eye*, p. 61. My italics. After 2-1-3, this 1-3-2 pattern seems next most frequent, for example:
    *h*ollows and *h*eights of *t*ime

    *p*iercing and *p*reying *a*che
    (*Ada*, pp.198, 281, respectively: my italics.)
30. Nabokov, *The Defense*, p. 227. My italics.
31. Nabokov, *The Gift*, p. 142. My italics.
32. Nabokov, *The Defense*, p. 59. My italics.
33. Nabokov, *Laughter in the Dark*, p. 26. My italics.
34. Nabokov, *Eugene Onegin*, Vol. III, p. 324. My italics.
35. Nabokov, *King, Queen, Knave*, p. 3. My italics.
36. Nabokov, *The Gift*, p. 24. My italics.
37. *Ibid.*, p. 29. My italics.
38. *Ibid.*, p. 363. My italics.
39. Nabokov, *Eugene Onegin*, Vol. III, p. 290. My italics.
40. *Ibid.*, p. 324. My italics.
41. Nabokov, *Despair*, p. 150. My italics.
42. If we include visual effects, still another variation may be found. For example, in Nabokov's translation of an expunged stanza from *Onegin's Journey:*

    be*st*illed is the re*bell*ious *bell*. . . .
    (Nabokov, *Eugene Onegin*, Vol. III, p. 261: my italics)

    Thus repeated, the "bell" does seem to rebell, seems barely bestilled. The visual pattern is now 1-2-3-3, or 2-1-2-3-3, if the preceding line is given:

    Quelled are its squares: midst them
    bestilled is the rebellious bell. . . .

    Yet another subpattern of juggled repetition is formed by "*its* . . . mi*dst* . . . be*st*illed *is* the."
    Consider also:

    *re*peating this *per*formance as much as *f*orty times. . . .

    (*Ibid.*, Vol. II, p. 299; my italics)

    wherein a slightly altered 1-3-2 pattern visually promotes the described repetition.
43. Such effects may well occur more often in Nabokov's English than in his Russian.

    In revising translations of his Russian novels he often sacrifices Strict literalness to euphony.

    (Proffer, pp. 148-9)

# 4.

## *Reader Participation*

Recalling Nabokov's lectures on literature at Cornell, Ross Wetzsteon has written that

> . . . in a gambit he was to use as many as three or four times a term, he would refer to "the passion of the scientist and the precision of the artist," pause for a moment as if he hadn't heard himself quite right, then ask in a mock-baffled tone: "Have I made a mistake? Don't I mean 'the passion of the artist and the precision of the scientist'?" Another pause, peering gleefully over the rims of his glasses, as if awaiting our answer—then "No! The passion of the scientist and the precision of the artist!" [1]

Other favored phrases were "Caress the details" and "the divine details." [2]

Introducing his translation of *Eugene Onegin,* Nabokov his written:

> In art as in science there is no delight without the detail, and it is on details that I have tried to fix the reader's attention.[3]

In his own fiction Nabokov also fixes the reader's attention on details—highly evocative details that enlist the reader's participation in creating the total effect. Precision of detail is thus of the essence, and we recall Nabokov's statement that "mere forms of speech" in Gogol "give rise to live creatures." [4]

But Nabokov is perhaps unsurpassed at limiting himself to a bare minimum of suggestive detail. Humbert Humbert, for example, imagines "so well" from a stark printed list "the colorful classroom," as he puts it, around Lolita:

> Grace and her ripe pimples; Ginny and her lagging leg; Gordon, the haggard masturbator; Duncan, the foul-smelling clown; nail-biting Agnes; Viola, of the blackheads and the bouncing bust; pretty Rosaline; dark Mary Rose; adorable Stella, who has let strangers touch her; Ralph, who bullies and steals; Irving for whom I am sorry.[5]

The "colorful classroom" springs to life through a minimum of highly strategic detail. And not only do these details evoke many others, the final images seem to fit surprisingly well their names on the previously given class list.[6] When the reader has pictured Gordon, he can return to the list and find that Gordon "is" Gordon. And when he has fully pictured Irving—of whom not a single specific is given—he has learned surprisingly much about Humbert Humbert. And even though the students are imagined by the narrator, the reader, who has helped, finds them very "real" indeed.

Parentheses sometimes enclose Nabokov's strategic details. Near the close of his "Pale Fire" Commentary Kinbote briefly dreams of what his next project may be: "I may join forces with Odon in a new motion picture: *Escape from Zembla* (ball in the palace, bomb in the palace square)." [7] The reader's initial image of the palace is extended to the square by the simple repetition of the word "palace." And the total, final vision even includes an inferred disruption of the original ball image.

A mere two words occasionally suffice. Early in *Lolita* Humbert reviews his past: "My very photogenic mother died in a freak accident (picnic, lightning) when I was three. . . ." [8]

Strategic detail often contributes to Nabokov's extensive and versatile technique of promoting the reader's creative participation. Most simply and most obviously, an image is described by means of its reflection, and the reader is left to construct the original. In *Speak, Memory,* Nabokov as a boy plays cards with his mother beside a window on a speeding train:

> Through forest and field, and in sudden ravines, and among scuttling cottages, those discarnate gamblers kept steadily playing on for steadily sparkling stakes.[9]

Just as he must transfer motion from "scuttling" cottages to speeding train, so the reader must reconstruct the "discarnate" gamblers inside the car. The same technique functions throughout the opening twelve lines of "Pale Fire," where the reader must recover the contents of Shade's room from the winter-night lawn outside and transfer the sky from his window pane to its rightful location.

In *Despair* Hermann tells us that "two enlaced birches looked at themselves in the water . . . "[10] and the reader must simply but vividly exchange "reality" and reflection. The image of a falling petal "shed by a blossoming tree" in *Speak, Memory* is startlingly reinforced by its own watery reflection, "which swiftly —more swiftly than the petal fell—rose to meet it. . . ."[11] After first meeting the tramp Felix, Hermann relates:

> When at last I got back to my hotel room, I found there, amid mercurial shadows and framed in frizzly bronze, Felix awaiting me. Pale-faced and solemn he drew near. He was now well-shaven; his hair was smoothly brushed back. He wore a dove-grey suit with a lilac tie. I took out my handkerchief; he took out his handkerchief too. A truce, parleying. . . . I . . . sat down on the edge of the bed, continuing the while to consult the mirror.[12]

With slight variations, Nabokov uses this device twice in *The Eye.*[13] Here, *mercurial* and *framed* subtly introduce the deception.

Since the reader himself must transfer the reflected detail from a false Felix to Hermann, the latter is perhaps the more effectively described. The word *mirror* may seem a somewhat heavyhanded touch, but few readers will note that the entire ruse was previewed three pages earlier, as well as on the preceding page where Hermann said he shook hands with Felix "only because it provided me with the curious sensation of Narcissus fooling Nemesis by helping his image out of the brook." Hermann has an amusingly belabored fascination for mirrors,[14] and Kinbote claims "in a sense" to have killed himself (*Kinbote* means *regicide* in Zemblan) by sinking "his identity in the mirror of exile."[15]

Such evocative reflections can be quite complex. In *Speak, Memory* the image of "a sullen day sitting for its picture in a puddle" is immediately reinforced by a series of evocative details that Nabokov "would deduce" from the "watery pallor" of a line of dull light entering his room between the white inner shutters.[16] Of Pnin's ophthalmologist father's waiting room we are told that

> . . . the blue dab of a window in miniature was reflected in the glass dome of an ormolu clock on the mantlepiece, and two flies kept describing slow quadrangles around the lifeless chandelier.[17]

The reader envisions this scene more precisely by having to strain his mind's eye—first to make out the miniature reflected window on the clock dome and then to focus on the pendulous structure framed by the flies. With very faint irony, *lifeless* gives body to the chandelier.

A "counterfeit king" in *Pale Fire*—presumably one of the many who helped the King escape—vividly appears as the real King's apparent reflection in a lake, yet his existence is limited to this reflection.[18] Reflections are imagined in *Pale Fire* when the King's supporters envision his escape by a motorboat kept in a coastal cave:

> . . . the imagined reflections of the trembling transparent water on rock wall and boat were tantalizing. . . .[19]

Other imagined reflections are described in *The Real Life of Sebastian Knight*,[20] and in *The Defense,* after Luzhin's imploring proposal of marriage:

> . . . she made an imaginary Luzhin enter the rooms, talk with her mother, eat home-cooked kulebiaka and be reflected in the sumptuous samovar purchased abroad. . . .[21]

Nabokovian shadows function similarly. Kinbote (who remarks that "our shadows still walk with us") paranoically imagines "death's fearful shadow" from the nocturnal sounds of cars and trucks: "would that shadow pull up at my door?"[22] The reader must supply the ominous vehicles themselves, which Kinbote proceeds by inference to fill with "phantom thugs." Also in the *Pale Fire* Commentary a "black shadow" walks into the "roses and thorns" of a garden and then materializes, quite appropriately, as a minister, whom the reader then easily clothes.[23] Notice also how a presumable nymphet springs to life in *Lolita:* "The grocer opposite had a little daughter whose shadow drove me mad. . . ."[24] (The key words "sh*adow* drove m*ad*" form a highly evocative 3-2-1 sound pattern.)

Such suggestive shadows can also be quite complex. In the poem "Pale Fire" Shade writes, of a hickory tree:

> White butterflies turn lavender as they
> Pass through its shade where gently seems to sway
> The phantom of my little daughter's swing.[25]

The darkening of butterflies helps the reader to picture the tree's shadow and hence the tree itself. Less obviously, a large solid hickory branch reaches out to suspend the imagined swaying swing.

In *The Defense* we see a painting wherein a shadow vividly reinforces an image already described:

> A village girl in a red kerchief coming down to her eyebrows

was eating an apple, and her black shadow on a fence was eating a slightly larger apple.[26]

Nabokov also promotes the reader's creative participation by means of suggested extensions and projections. The resulting inferred images can be "real" or purely imaginary. In "The Visit to the Museum" the custodian has "one hand behind his back and the ghost of the other in his pocket. . . ."[27] A painting in "The Vane Sisters" called "Seen Through a Windshield" depicts "a windshield partly covered with rime, with a brilliant trickle (from an imaginary car roof) across its transparent part. . . ."[28] Here, the reader's eye is vividly led beyond its own area of focus with the result of further sharpening this same area. In *Pnin* a cartoon is described wherein—as "puffs" above their heads reveal—a sailor imagines a mermaid "as having a pair of legs" and a cat imagines her "as all fish."[29]

The device functions especially evocatively in *Pale Fire*. As Gradus prepares to close in for the kill, Kinbote supposes that "the forward projection of what imagination he had, stopped at the act, on the brink of all its possible consequences;

> ghost consequences, comparable to the ghost toes of an amputee or to the fanning out of additional squares which a chess knight (that skip-space piece), standing on a marginal file, "feels" in phantom extensions beyond the board, but which have no effect whatever on his real moves, on the real play."[30]

"Ghostly" words such as *phantom, discarnate, invisible, imaginary,* and *spectral* often promote such effects.

More generally, the device may be seen as a variation of Nabokov's major descriptive technique of coloring the "real" and the "unreal" with tints of each other.

Both these "coloring" methods typically compel the reader to adjust his perspective and to focus in more closely, but the real is tinctured by the unreal somewhat less often. In *Speak,*

*Memory,* for example, Nabokov tells how his father, leaving the family at luncheon, would go outside to meet his peasants:

> . . . the courteous buzz of a peasant welcome would reach us as the invisible group greeted my invisible father.[31]

From the young Nabokov's place at table, he could see through the window "a marvelous case of levitation."

> There, for an instant, the figure of my father would be displayed, gloriously sprawling in midair, his limbs in a curiously casual attitude, his handsome, imperturbable features turned to the sky. Thrice, to the mighty heave-ho of his invisible tossers, he would fly up in this fashion. . . .

Aided by evocative detail and suggestive sound effects, the reader almost involuntarily transforms the "invisible" (group, father, tossers) into the vividly visible. In *The Real Life of Sebastian Knight* we read that "invisible cattle lowed sadly in some shunted truck. . . ."[32] As above, the word *invisible* tends to mute an object the reader must clarify.

Such "ghostly" colorings of the real by the unreal are often attributable to physical or psychic causes. Early in *King, Queen, Knave* Franz breaks his glasses. His ensuing perceptions include "vague hostile objects," a "clowning mirror," "the yellow mirage of a bus," "a faceless traveller," "a cloudy passer-by," and "the specter of a dog."[33]

While going mad, Luzhin *(The Defense)* encounters numerous "phantoms" and "ghosts"[34] that picturesquely suggest a consciousness wildly producing possible chess moves and only very vaguely perceiving its palpable surroundings. Smurov *(The Eye)* "good-naturedly yields" to illusions that include "a spectral hospital ward," city streets that "greatly resembled reality," "Russian books instantly printed to humor" him, and even himself—whom he observes "like an inexperienced ghost," although he does "catch his imagination" in the "inaccuracy" of removing another's mustache.[35]

Hermann *(Despair)* dwells at length on an "aberration" he has, "a well-known kind of 'dissociation,' " whereby he observes himself making love to his wife from vantage points that grow ever more remote.[36] At the height of his "detachment," Hermann's imaginary double retires to the parlor and watches, in the mirror on an open wardrobe, the side show of his own reflected bed.

The unreal is colored by the real more frequently.[37] "Ghostly" words such as "invisible" are effective in these instances as well. Suggesting that Lolita's "drives" should fall into a "rounded pattern," Miss Pratt's "hands held for a moment an invisible melon." [38] Here the reader must subdue the "unreal" melon in order to visualize the "real" hands properly spaced in "real" air.

After Humbert has experienced a climax with the apparently unsuspecting Lolita on his lap, he adds:

> What I had madly possessed was not she, but my own creation, another fanciful Lolita—perhaps more real than Lolita; overlapping, encasing her; floating between me and her, and having no will, no consciousness—indeed, no life of her own.[39]

So real, it seems, has this imagined Lolita become, and so "close" to the real one ("overlapping, encasing")—that Humbert can safely remind us she had "no life of her own;" safely, moreover, because the reader is thus subtly invited to defend the very life-like image he has just been induced to share with Humbert.

In *Speak, Memory* Nabokov as a youth "would lie awake and imagine all kinds of romantic situations. . . ."

> . . . a sleek ruffian . . . was holding her by the wrist and interrogating her with a crooked grin, . . . and the following night he was shot, lassoed, buried alive, shot again, throttled, bitingly insulted, coolly aimed at, spared, and left to drag out a life of shame.[40]

Note that the extinguished life is both revived and even subjected to a painful prolongation.

Desire for another's death provides Nabokov with an ideal vehicle for painting the unreal in real colors. Plotting to kill Dreyer, Franz repeatedly terms him "the deceased" and Martha dubs him "my late husband." [41] During a four-page rhapsody of ways to murder Dreyer, a second method derives some of its vividness from the preceding imagined one. Franz, we read, "would be waiting behind the tree with the reloaded revolver." [42] Relentlessly, and perhaps for the reader who failed to notice "reloaded," the next sentence begins: "When they had again killed him, . . ."

After Charlotte's death, Humbert schemes to "whizz over to camp Q., tell Lolita her mother was about to undergo a major operation in an invented hospital,

> and then keep moving with my sleepy nymphet from inn to inn while her mother got better and better and finally died." [43]

The word *inn* is a typical Nabokovian very casual potential sexual pun. Its repetition, and the attendant brisk implication that virtually nothing else would occur, both add to the fun. *Sleepy* helps too.

A variation of treating the unreal as real turns on word order. A person or thing is first referred to as real and then *(logically)* erased. For instance, Nabokov describes himself in *Speak, Memory* as awaiting "a certain stone-faced pupil, who would *always* turn up despite the obstacles I mentally piled in his way. . . ." [44] "Mentally" does most of the erasing. Later, Nabokov describes the first poem he composed: "As I carried it homeward, still unwritten. . . ." [45] *Unwritten* (which erases "it") alters the meaning of *carried* and intensifies, with the reader's help, the reality of the poem.

Franz's landlord presumes that Franz goes to work every day, and so he decides he has "no alternative but to leave the house for the whole day in order to perform the job that the old fellow had invented for him. . . ." [46] The reader seems subtly invited to invent the job for the old fellow. When Martha calls on Franz:

> He covered his bare Adam's apple with his hand and uttered a long sentence but noticed with surprise that seemingly no words had been produced, as if he had tapped them out on a typewriter in which he had forgotten to insert a ribbon.[47]

The "uttered" words last unusually long before they are erased.

Combinations of real and unreal colorings occasionally occur. As Gradus flies closer, Kinbote remarks: ". . . head-on but quite safely, phantom-like, we pass through him, through the shimmering propeller of his flying machine. . . ." [48] This device (of rendering Gradus more "real" by making us less) seems the more remarkable since Kinbote is presumably imagining the entire story. (In which case, he is here imagining what his imagined killer might be doing.)

Finally, Nabokov telescopes time by treating the ("unreal") past or future as if it were at least partially ("real") present. Pnin for instance reminiscently removes his glasses "to beam at the past while massaging the lenses of the present." [49] Luzhin's wife "bent forward to see her future . . . the same, sullen, bowed Luzhin. . . ." [50] and "set off into Luzhin's past, dragging Valentinov with her, visualizing him. . . ." [51] In *The Gift* Fyodor imagines his father's past, complete with the latter's probable (subsequent but also past) recollections thereof, and even describes his father's reaction to these various imagined recollections.[52] And in *King, Queen, Knave* we read that "At least two future stories of the new corner house could be discerned through the scaffolding of the present." [53]

Returning to Nabokov's assertion that "there is no delight without the detail," it becomes evident that the reader's delight must be earned. Strategic reflections, shadows, extensions, projections, a faint coloring of the real by the unreal, and especially vice versa—all contribute, together with highly suggestive detail, to promoting the reader's creative participation.[54] Thus involuntarily engaged however, the reader enjoys a vivid, creative experience rather than a passive, stock response.

## *Notes*

1. Ross Wetzsteon, "Nabokov as teacher," *Triquarterly* (Winter, 1970), p. 242.
2. *Ibid.*, p. 245.
   In a recent conversation Nabokov spoke of "those gusty little details" in the first part of Rousseau's *Confessions*.
   He has also recently spoken about "such combinations of details as yield the sensual spark without which a book is dead." ["Vladimir Nabokov Talks About Nabokov," *Vogue* (December, 1969), p. 191.]
3. Vladimir Nabokov, *Eugene Onegin* (New York, 1964), vol. I, p. 8.
4. Vladimir Nabokov, *Nikolai Gogol* (New York, 1944), p. 78.
   A "seedy and touchy" little official in *The Defense* who "was eating a diabetic roll" is described as follows:

   > He probably received a miserable salary, was married and had a child whose whole body was covered with a rash.

   (Vladimir Nabokov, *The Defense*, New York, 1964, p. 224)

   Here the reader is led, by means of evocative detail, to picture with greater clarity the very person from which the detail allegedly derived. The resulting vivid, haunting return is most Gogolian.
5. Vladimir Nabokov, *Lolita* (New York, 1959), pp. 50-1.
6. Nabokov admits recalling this list with "special delectation." (*Ibid.*, p. 318).
7. Vladimir Nabokov, *Pale Fire* (New York, 1966), p. 212.
8. Nabokov, *Lolita*, p. 12.
9. Vladimir Nabokov, *Speak, Memory* (New York, 1966), pp. 142-3.
10. Vladimir Nabokov, *Despair* (New York, 1966), p. 49.
11. Nabokov, *Speak, Memory*, pp. 270-1.
12. Nabokov, *Despair*, p. 24.
13. Vladimir Nabokov, *The Eye* (New York, 1966), pp. 17, 104.
14. See especially Nabokov, *Despair*, pp. 34, 74.
15. Nabokov, *Pale Fire*, p. 189.
16. Nabokov, *Speak, Memory*, p. 119.
17. Vladimir Nabokov, *Pnin* (New York, 1965), p. 175.
18. Nabokov, *Pale Fire*, p. 103.
19. *Ibid.*, p. 87.
20. Vladimir Nabokov, *The Real Life of Sebastian Knight* (Norfolk, Conn., 1959), pp. 137-8.
21. Nabokov, *The Defense*, p. 101.
22. Nabokov, *Pale Fire*, pp. 8, 70.

23. *Ibid.*, p. 64.
24. Nabokov, *Lolita*, p. 27.
25. *Ibid.*, p. 24.
26. Nabokov, *The Defense*, p. 118.
27. *Nabokov's Quartet* (New York, 1966), p. 94.
28. *Ibid.*, p. 81.
29. Nabokov, *Pnin*, p. 61.
30. Nabokov, *Pale Fire*, p. 195.
31. Nabokov, *Speak, Memory*, p. 31.
32. Nabokov, *The Real Life of Sebastian Knight*, p. 121.
33. Vladimir Nabokov, *King, Queen, Knave* (New York, 1968), pp. 22-9.
34. Nabokov, *The Defense*, pp. 138-9.
35. Nabokov, *The Eye*, pp. 21-4.
36. Nabokov, *Despair*, pp. 37-9.
37. In addition to the passages discussed below, please see Appendix C.
38. Nabokov, *Lolita*, p. 177.
39. *Ibid.*, p. 59. See also pp. 22, 60.
40. Nabokov, *Speak, Memory*, p. 206.
41. Nabokov, *King, Queen, Knave*, p. 156.
42. *Ibid.*, p. 179.
43. Nabokov, *Lolita*, p. 98.
44. Nabokov, *Speak, Memory*, p. 88.
45. *Ibid.*, p. 225.
46. Nabokov, *King, Queen, Knave*, p. 57.
47. *Ibid.*, p. 95. He also "soundlessly" tells a bus conductor his inner feelings (*ibid.*, p. 85).
48. Nabokov, *Pale Fire*, p. 196.
49. Nabokov, *Pnin*, p. 11.
50. Nabokov, *The Defense*, p. 233.
51. *Ibid.*, p. 238.
52. Vladimir Nabokov, *The Gift* (New York, 1963), p. 136.
53. Nabokov, *King, Queen, Knave*, p. 52.
54. Writing about what he terms Nabokov's "patterned works," Quentin Anderson has gone so far as to claim: "If you are persuaded you are reading a full-fledged novelist you are unaware of your collaboration." ["Nabokov in Time," *The New Republic* (June 4, 1966), p. 28.]

# 5.

## "Reality"

Nabokov employs several devices that tend to create a reciprocal relationship between the real and the unreal. As a result, illusion seems subtly to permeate and to expand the world we normally take for granted. Some of the methods seem rather scornfully to undermine "reality" but are in fact a special brand of Romantic irony calculated to entice the reader into sympathy with various effects exposed by the author. And perhaps mad Kinbote speaks partly as Nabokov when he mentions "the basic fact" that

> "reality" is neither the subject nor the object of true art which creates its own special reality having nothing to do with the average "reality" perceived by the communal eye.[1]

Nabokov often intrudes upon his narration with the sole apparent purpose of stressing its artificial nature. At times he even begins a description in this way. Chapter Eight of *Speak, Memory* opens: "I am going to show a few slides, but first let me indicate the where and the when of the matter." [2] The reader, promised a coming show, is content to sit back and wait. More important, he has been led to expect "only" an artificial demonstration; Nabokov's careful selection of vividly evocative detail is then pleasantly refreshing. And the effect feeds constructively upon itself. A few pages later, a paragraph abruptly begins:

> The next picture looks as if it had come on the screen upside down. It shows our third tutor standing on his head. He was a . . .[3]

Almost involuntarily, the reader strains to see the very screen he has himself been induced to imagine. There is little time to marvel at how we have been inveigled into accepting the "reality" of the avowedly unreal: Nabokov quickly supplies a series of sharp, bright details. But how less vivid they might seem, perhaps, had the paragraph blandly begun: "Our third tutor was a . . ."

*Laughter in the Dark* opens with a short, disarming plot summary labeled "the whole of the story." [4] The reader thus learns all, and yet almost nothing, of what will follow. He is then offered the pleasant surprise that so much can be made from so little. And this, one can infer, is an effect not unsavored by Nabokov.

Speciously exposing his own artifice, Nabokov ends *Laughter* with "stage directions for last silent scene: . . ." [5] *Invitation to a Beheading* concludes with "everything coming apart" and the "scenery flapping." [6] *The Real Life of Sebastian Knight* ends with a reference to "a lighted stage" and a "bald little prompter" who "shuts his book." [7] Hermann's climactic murder scene is accompanied by a "crash of cymbals in the orchestra" in parentheses.[8]

The effect may occur at any point within the work. Chapter Three of *Despair* opens: "How shall I begin this chapter? I offer several variations to choose from." (Actually, this is itself a deception: portions of all three given variations instructively linger, both their "what" and their "how" contributing significantly to the total effect.)

Parenthetical intrusions are frequent. In *Laughter* Albinus rattles the handle of a door behind which Margot and Rex are deceiving him: "(. . . quite unconscious of the queer part doors played in his and her life)." [9] Later: "No, there was no key (doors were always against him)." [10] Doors are most important in the novel,[11] and such remarks both tend to excuse the theme's contrivance and alert the reader to the tortuous fun of following its intricate development. Mirrors are also speciously abused, as in *Laughter*: ". . . (mirrors were having plenty of work that day) . . ."; [12] or in *King, Queen, Knave*: "The looking glass, which was working hard that night, reflected. . . ." [13]

At times, Nabokov's "obvious" revelations of his own narrational techniques seem little more than playful self-indulgence. But even the fun with "McFate" [14] in *Lolita* and Humbert's decision to give his readers' "imaginations a kick in the pants" [15] both serve the purpose of pointing up the narrator's delightfully treacherous selection of what we are told. Moreover such attitudes subtly insinuate, albeit humorously, that unknown forces are perhaps constantly at work behind "reality"—forces possibly better left unknown.

Nabokov often reverses normally accepted patterns. Typically, his book on Gogol opens with the latter's death and ends with his birth [16]; and the map Nabokov specially prepared for *Speak, Memory* has "North" at the bottom, "South" at the top. The narrator of *Pnin* begins his last chapter: "My first recollection of Timofey Pnin . . . ," [17] and the book ends with an imitation of a scene prefigured in its beginning. As a result, "reality" assumes for the reader an elusive quality of circular timelessness. "I confess," Nabokov has asserted, "I do not believe in time." [18]

The sense of timelessness in Nabokov's works also derives from carefully controlled echoes. A tiny detail, a shape, a vivid little phrase will appear and reappear—*almost* unnoticed. The present is thus subtly colored by the past, and the reader himself tends to experience and reexperience the story within its own perceptual framework. And the future is continually prefigured. Time becomes a series of superimposed translucent layers, shifting just enough to reveal unexpected, familiar glimpses. Such echoes, which often range across hundreds of pages, can be almost diabolically teasing. They suggest, unsettlingly, that an entire novel is perceived by Someone as a single moment of alien but logically telescoped time. For example Humbert vividly reevokes his unfortunate seaside love scene which was interrupted by "exclamations of ribald encouragement" [19] as he abruptly digresses: "Those ribald sea monsters." [20] This time he goes on to quote the exclamations, and even inferentially evokes the image of naked Annabel ("trying to screen her"), but the echo of "ribald" has already touched off, in the alert reader, a replay of the earlier scene.

As Dabney Stuart has shown, much of the plot development in *Laughter in the Dark* is foreshadowed during its opening pages, and especially by two briefly described scenes in a movie Albinus watches.[21] The device is typical. Early in *Despair* Hermann mentions that he and his "double" Felix are "as alike as two drops of blood." [22] When he at last explains his murder plan to Lydia,[23] Hermann says: "We resemble each other, don't interrupt, like two drops of blood, and he'll be particuarly like me when dead." Similarly, Hermann describes himself as "slashing his knee with a yellow glove" [24] when he first meets Felix; just before the murder, we see him "slashing myself with the glove still more furiously." [25] More subtly, the murder is prefigured by Hermann's initial impression of Felix: "the emphasis of that immobility, the lifelessness of those widespread legs, the stiffness of that half-bent arm" [26]; less subtly, by the way he keeps picturing himself the next night: "in the sorry guise of a tramp, his face motionless, with chin and cheeks bristle-shaded, as happens to a dead man overnight" [27]; and even less subtly by his remembering, months later, that he had seen "a tramp asleep on the grass who exactly resembled my corpse." [28]

Dreyer's "drowning" at the end of *King, Queen, Knave* is constantly, relentlessly prefigured. The hints range in obviousness from relatively subtle puns ("how can one *poor relation swamp* anything" [29]) to explicit references to drowning.[30]

*The Defense* contains an intricate network of echoes that help to prefigure Luzhin's impending madness, and words relating to music and harmony are especially frequent.[31] Such terms are similarly employed in *Pale Fire*. Kinbote's amusing symptoms of sweet bells jangled include the sudden and very loud amusement park [32] whose music plagues him [33] but which does not exist,[34] although it echoes as "that carrousel inside and outside my head." [35]

Nabokov's English version of "The Potato-Elf" (a Russian story written in 1929) contains several typical echoes. Fred, a fleshy-nosed dwarf greatly in need of a female dwarf, finally achieves sexual satisfaction with Nora, a normal-sized married woman, even though, in his shyness, he cannot "tear his gaze from the green pom-pom" on her slipper.[36] (This strangely inter-echoes, as often happens in Nabokov's world, with the pompom slippers that echoingly represent sexual intercourse in *King, Queens, Knave*.[37])

When Fred and Nora are first brought together, she is "tapping her nails against the glass of a fish bowl, where several goldfish, which looked as if they were carved out of orange peel, were gently breathing. . . ."[38] After Fred's happiness, he learns that Nora has no desire to accommodate him further, and his life grows lonely and sad. Eight years later a woman in black with a familiar voice calls on Fred, who, we read, "remembered very vividly the orange fish in the glass bowl."[39] She is described, they exchange awkward greetings, and:

> "Is it possible that she again . . . ?" thought the dwarf abruptly. In his thoughts he saw again with rushing swiftness —the bowl with the fish—the smell of eau de cologne—the emerald pom-pom on the slipper.
> Nora got up. The gloves fell on the floor like two little black balls.

Fred's hopes re-evoke for the reader the scene of his previous success. More subtly, the phrase "with rushing swiftness" faintly parallels the only direct description of their former love-making: ". . . suddenly, absurdly, and delightfully—everything became motion."[40]

But Nora, it develops, has merely come to announce that she has had a child by Fred. She rises, picks up her "sticky black balls of gloves," assures the stunned Fred that his son is "as big as other boys," and leaves.[41] Soon regaining his senses, he runs a long way after her, collapsing at her feet like "a crumpled black glove."[42] The story then ends with Nora saying: "I know nothing about this. . . . My son died a short time ago. . . ." Thus, the *black glove* echoes are themselves signal echoes of her being dressed "in black"—echoes which end with Fred's crumpled position, the fact of his "new" son's death, and Fred's apparent death as well ("Someone, understanding that this was not all a joke, bent over the dwarf, whistled softly and took off his cap.").

"The Potato-Elf" contains several other similar but relatively minor evocative echoes. A Spanish dancer's legs, for example, symbolize Fred's initial lust,[43] echo his success,[44] and can even be seen, as those of a "Russian ballerina," [45] to prefigure his hopes that Nora has returned for more. "Aromatic alcohol" is echoed by Nora's "aromatic, cool hands," [46] and the dwarf's happiness seems subtly re-evoked by the echo of his "mouse-colored spats." [47]

It should be emphasized that in context such little touches are both more subtle and more suggestive. Even less-careful readers presumably experience a vague, atmospheric recognition as a piece of familiar scenery flashes past.

Nabokov often utilizes inanimate objects, backgrounds, and events to reflect his characters' mental and emotional states. The result is a calculated, vivid exploitation of the pathetic fallacy. Indeed, with his own special brand of Romantic irony Nabokov typically assures the reader that he, Nabokov, is fully aware of what he is doing. Humbert Humbert picks up Rita (his post-Lolita partner) "one *depraved* May evening": "she would have given herself," he punnishly hazards, "to any pathetic creature or fallacy. . . ." [48]

Humbert first sees Lolita in a "breathless" garden.[49] When Charlotte has read his diary, taken from a "raped" little table,[50] he decides to fix her a calming drink and opens the refrigerator: "It roared at me viciously while I removed the ice from its heart." [51] (Here Nabokov expands the effect to monster-like personification.) Such descriptions typically reflect feverish emotional states and logically increase in frequency as *Lolita* progresses.

Once, after climbing a mountain to where "a last panting pine was taking a well-earned breather on the rock it had reached," Lolita and Humbert are surprised immediately after making love:

Alas, I had not reckoned with a faint side trail
that curled up in *cagey* fashion among the shrubs and rocks a
few feet from us.[52]

Like most of Nabokov's fiction, *Lolita* is generously laced with emotion-reflecting modifiers. Lolita herself, for example, fills with her own "rosy" sunshine a "surprised and pleased closet-door mirror."[53] Later, she and Humbert suddenly leave town and drive away from their "puzzled" house.[54] And—always at most appropriate moments—Humbert tells us he crowded the demons of his desire against a "throbbing" balcony,[55] drank from a "friendly" flask,[56] practiced killing a sweater in a "speechless" (note the pun) glade,[57] drove in an "almost cheerfully working" car,[58] and shot a rocking chair that rocked "in a panic all by itself."[59] (Twenty-five pages earlier, with prophetic irony, Humbert had sat "in this subdued, frightened-to-death rocking chair.") Nor are emotions reflected exclusively in inanimate backgrounds. Humbert finally gives Lolita her money, even offering to buy the old car for five hundred dollars:

> "At this rate we'll be millionnaires next," she said to the ecstatic dog.[60]

Sudden noises, especially at dramatic moments, provide an ideal and frequent vehicle for such projected, or reflected, emotions. Humbert tells us that the day he was to visit Dolly Schiller he disarmed his alarm clock before it "exploded."[61] When he pressed her door bell, "it vibrated through my whole system."[62] He finally arrives to kill Quilty: the sun

> was burning like a man, and the birds screamed in the drenched and steaming trees. . . .
> A guardedly ironic silence answered my bell.[63]

Here, even the lack of sound is endowed with reflected emotion; "screamed" is more typical.

But Nabokov's favorite such noise is the eloquent ringing of a telephone. For example, Hermann *(Despair)* feverishly tells us that he

> . . . sat down, pressed my temples. Suddenly, mad with fury, the telephone rang.[64]

Incidentally, sparrows reflect Hermann's fear [65] much as the birds "screamed" at murderous Humbert. And, as Hermann prepares to shoot his victim, he slams the car door "with a bang that was louder than any shot." [66] Later he mentions "a mercilessly blue sky," [67] which can be seen to inter-echo with the perceptions of jealous Humbert, who looks up at "the smiling plotting sky" —at a moment when he supposes that even "the idiotic green love birds in a cage . . . were in the plot, the sordid plot." [68] Humbert's suspicions are even reflected in "a conspiracy of poplars." [69]

This almost paranoic mode of perception suggests the Nabokovian phenomenon of "referential mania." This designation is defined in a short story of 1948 called "Signs and Symbols."

> . . . the patient imagines that everything happening around him is a veiled reference to his personality and existence.[70]

Because he considers himself so more intelligent than "other men," Nabokov continues, the patient excludes "real people" (note the Gogolian adjective) from the "conspiracy."

> Clouds in the *staring* sky transmit to one another, by means of *slow* signs, *incredibly* detailed information regarding him. His inmost thoughts are discussed at nightfall, in manual alphabet, by *darkly* gesticulating trees. Pebbles or stains or sun flecks form patterns representing *in some awful way* messages which he must intercept.[71]

The feeling of perpetual uneasiness conveyed by *staring* is made both ominous and agonizing by *slow*. "Incredibly detailed" (rather than "incredibly transmit") subtly takes us deep within the demented mind. (This description of "his" point of view is thus given partially *from* his point of view.) *Darkly,* as a pun (the night or the "conspiracy"), serves to support and embellish *both* narrational vantage points. Similarly, the phrase "in some awful way" can be seen to apply not only to the patient's fears but even to the reader's horror upon envisioning them.[72]

Andrew Field has appropriately linked this patient with Luzhin *(The Defense)*.[73] As he gradually goes mad, Luzhin perceives more and more clearly a chesslike attack in all that surrounds him—an attack against which he presumably "defends" himself through suicide.

Less than halfway through the novel, Luzhin gloomily shrugs his shoulders looking at the floor,

> where a slight movement was taking place *perceptible* to him alone, an evil differentiation of shadows. . . . Having stamped out a shadow in one place, Luzhin saw with despair that *far from where he was sitting* a new combination was taking shape on the floor.[74]

"The patient's" superiority to "other men" is stressed by *alone*. There is also a light irony in the emphasis of physical distance between Luzhin and the newly forming pattern. On the next page the conspiratorial shadows become "so brazen" that Luzhin "involuntarily" (note the reflex-like reaction to his own fantasy) reaches out to move imaginary chessmen.

Luzhin's illusions grow more and more "brazen" until, late in the novel:

> A lull, thought Luzhin that day. A lull but with hidden preparations. It wants to take me unawares.[75]

Note the subtle but viciously circular irony of Luzhin's awareness that his imagined "it" wants to take him unawares.

The "lull" then continues "for two or three days" and includes a visit to a dentist, who hands Luzhin an ordinary tooth chart:

> There was nothing suspicious in all this and the cunning lull continued until Thursday.

Even the absence of evidence has now become suspect.

Variations of referential mania appear in Nabokov's other works. Pnin's "tussle with the wallpaper," for example, centers on his trying to determine "what system of inclusion and circumspection governed the horizontal recurrence of the pattern."

> *It stood to reason* that if the evil designer—*the destroyer of minds,* the friend of fever—had concealed the key of the pattern with such monstrous care, that the key must be as precious as life itself . . .[76]

The two italicized phrases are in obviously ironic juxtaposition and subtly point up the self-defeating aspect of Pnin's very inspiration. Note also *monstrous.*

When Kinbote first gets hold of the poem "Pale Fire" he employs a simile of referential mania to describe his own emotions:

> . . . I found myself enriched with an indescribable amazement as if informed that fire-flies were making decodable signals on behalf of stranded spirits, or that a bat was writing a legible tale of torture in the bruised and branded sky.[77]

Not only do Nabokov's characters distortedly (but instructively) perceive *how* things happen; the reader is often subtly induced to draw premature, erroneous conclusions about *what* is taking place. The effect seems best explained in Nabokov's famous illustration:

> Uncle alone in the house with the children said he'd dress up to amuse them. After a long wait, as he did not appear, they went down and saw a masked man putting the table silver into a bag. "Oh, Uncle," they cried in delight. "Yes, isn't my make-up good?" said Uncle, taking his mask off. Thus goes the Hegelian syllogism of humor. Thesis: Uncle made himself up as a burglar (a laugh for the children); anthesis: it *was* a burglar (a laugh for the reader); synthesis: it still was Uncle (fooling the reader.) [78]

This passage from *Laughter in the Dark* explains Axel Rex's special brand of humor and illuminates some of the mechanism behind Nabokov's deception.

Many of Nabokov's narrational syllogisms turn on whether illicit lovers are to be surprised. In *Laughter* alone, for example, six of nine syllogisms are of this type.

When brazen Margot visits Albinus at home quite unexpectedly, there is considerable suspense as to whether her presence will be detected. Paul "by some miracle" failed to notice "the edge of a bright red frock" showing from behind a bookstand.[79] Albinus then silently prays that Margot will get "a chance of slipping out; if, indeed, she had that intention." Finally, his wife in bed, Albinus goes down in his pajamas to "read a bit." "In a moment, she will be mine," he imagines. Opening the library door, he "feverishly" whispers: "Margot, you mad little thing." "But it was only," the chapter ends,

> a scarlet silk cushion which he himself had brought there a few days ago, to crouch on while consulting Nonnenmacher's *History of Art*—ten volumes, folio.

Antithetically, we are led to believe Margot has further pranks in mind by the tiny twist of thought "if, indeed." This seed of doubt grows rapidly, thanks to Albinus' pajamas and feverish expectancy. Typically, it is Albinus himself who has innocently planted the cushion that deceives him. Note also that his own deception of going down to "read a bit" ironically foreshadows the folio.

Later, when Albinus finds the lovers suspiciously close, Rex "coolly" denies embracing Margot: "I was only making her comfortable and got entangled, you see." [80] (Humorously enough, his statement is entirely true.) "Come to my study," Albinus tells Rex "darkly." Then, "with a heavy frown," he proceeds to speak of something quite unrelated to our expectations.

Similar "amorous syllogisms" include the postman's delivery of Margot's rash letter to Albinus,[81] Margot's "deceiving" him,[82] and his suspenseful attempts to "stroke her head" late in the novel.[83] The Rouginard-bus-episode syllogism spans several pages and affords a prime example of prophetic irony.

Udo Conrad, the reader will recall, sits strategically behind Margot and Rex on the Rouginard bus, which Albinus has missed. Albinus learns this fact,[84] and then he calls on Conrad, totally unaware of what the latter could have overheard. The two converse at some length. Udo mentions the others' "merriment" at Albinus' plight, and Albinus considers, but decides against revealing his relationship with Margot. (Since this presumably would have triggered a premature synthesis, it can be deemed an illusory antithesis.) Both Udo and Albinus become "very bored," and the latter, leaving, ironically decides: "Catch me calling on him again!"

Within two pages, Albinus stumbles upon painfully suspicious evidence of Margot's deception and rushes directly back to call on Udo, who vividly confirms his very worst fears. "What did those two talk about on the bus?"

> ". . . it was the cheapest, loudest, nastiest amorous prattle that I've ever heard in my life. Those friends of yours talked as freely of their love as though they were alone in Paradise—a rather gross Paradise, I'm afraid." [85]

The special fun here seems to turn on the fact that the reader, in Albinus' own phrase, "catches him calling on" Udo all too soon after his ironically prophetic pronouncement.

Just as Albinus appears to suspect Margot and Rex, thus effecting the "come to my study" syllogism, Marina seems to suspect Ada and Van. When he attempts to pass it off, she explains that it was Van and *Lucette* to whom she had imputed incest.[86] Similarly, when Martha and Franz secretly hold hands at a theater (*King, Queen, Knave*), her husband Dreyer tells them to "let him know" when "this obscene abomination is over." [87] It soon develops that his reference was to the violin music. While Lolita and Humbert kiss, parked on a highway's shoulder, a policeman drives up to ask something quite unrelated to their embraces. Afterwards, Lo tells Humbert: "He should have nabbed you." [88]

Her reference, we soon learn, was to his speeding. In *Pale Fire,* Kinbote's department chairman questions him because "a boy had complained to his adviser." [89] The complaint, it develops, was totally unrelated to sexual advances. "Laughing in sheer relief," Kinbote embraces him and promises never to be "naughty" again. In relating this, he casually refers to his chairman (Dr. Nattochdag) as "my good Netochka." (In a work by Dostoevsky, *Netochka Nezvanova,* two very young girls, Netochka and Katya, hover vividly upon the brink of homosexual activities.)

Nabokov's syllogistic deceptions vary greatly in scope. A single sentence can suffice. After Humbert receives Lolita's letter requesting financial aid:

> At first I planned to drive all day and night, but then thought better of it and rested for a couple of hours around dawn in a motor court room, a few miles before reaching town.[90]

Despite the factual materialization here of antithesis ("thought better of it"), the final effect, or synthesis, seems almost humorously little removed from thesis, or original plan.

One of Nabokov's Russian short stories, "The Admiralty Needle" (Berlin, 1933), can be seen as a fifteen-page syllogism. A shorter one (the tale of Mr. X.Y.) is inserted by Hermann into *Despair;* [91] his "not mailing and yet mailing after all" a letter (with the help of a little girl) forms another,[92] and so on.

Syllogistic narration orders even the basic plots of Nabokov's novels. For instance, the reader of *Laughter in the Dark* is led to envision Albinus slowly regaining, but concealing, his sight— while Margot and Rex delight in deceiving him before his eyes. But no: he remains dutifully blind.

Similarly, we suspect that, despite the incompetence of their schemes, Martha and Franz may really drown Dreyer. Conversely, we wonder if Hermann, despite his crafty plans, will really accomplish the murder of his double. (Since the man he kills is not his double and since he bungles the deed by forgetting the walking stick, the synthesis is in a sense double.) And, as Carl Proffer has shown,[93] the "clever" reader of *Lolita* is carefully led to believe that Humbert will shoot his nymphet. (As John Ray, Jr. covertly explains in his Foreword, she actually dies in childbirth.)

Syllogistic development is basic to Nabokov's mode of thought and expression. What seems most vivid, bright and "real" is typically most certain to prove illusory or deceptive. Appearances, we suspect, may be calculated to punish mere cleverness—to turn it directly away from what is "real" like the antithetic arc of a spiral. In an often-quoted passage from *Speak, Memory* Nabokov says, of a chess problem he spent months composing:

> It was meant for the delectation of the very expert solver. The unsophisticated might miss the point of the problem entirely, and discover its fairly simple, "thetic" solution without having passed through the pleasurable torments prepared for the sophisticated one.[94]

In Nabokov's spiraling world, the completed syllogism leads the reader back to where he began, but with a disturbing insistence that he is now somewhere else. The components of "reality" are thus loosened from strict and static interconnection, and seem to float more freely.

> The spiral is a spiritualized circle. In the spiral form, the circle, uncoiled, unwound, has ceased to be vicious; it has been set free.[95]

This passage from *Speak, Memory* applies even to the relationship between "reality" and Nabokov's style. Nabokovian romantic ironies, echoings, pathetic fallacies, referential mania, syllogistic twists—all refreshingly undermine the structure of the conventional fictional world, freeing the reader to experience a plastic and consciousness-expanding "reality." The entire vivid display accorded human perception seems controlled by some alien and disturbingly playful Force. Perhaps not just "reality," we suspect, but our very perceptual process is a "clever" deception. One thinks of phenomenology and of Nabokov's recent (1969) statement:

... I tend more and more to regard the objective existence of *all* events as a form of impure imagination—hence my inverted commas around "reality." Whatever the mind grasps, it does so with the assistance of creative fancy, that drop of water on a glass slide, which gives distinctness and relief to the observed organism.[96]

Asked whether he believes in God, Nabokov has stated:

... I know more than I can express in words, and the little I can express would not have been expressed, had I not known more.[97]

The implication seems to be that there is something Nabokov knows and cannot say which is nevertheless the source of what he does say. Thus we can sense another world behind the printed word. And thus Nabokov has concluded his study of Gogol:

While trying to convey my attitude towards his art I have not produced any tangible proofs of its peculiar existence.[98]

Nabokovian "Reality"—too elusive and too large for direct expression—is suggested inferentially, intangibly, deceptively.

## Notes

1. Vladimir Nabokov, *Pale Fire* (New York, 1966), p. 94.
   Nabokov is of course famous for saying that "reality" is "one of the few words which mean nothing without quotes." (*Lolita*, New York, 1959, p. 283.)
2. Vladimir Nabokov, *Speak, Memory* (New York, 1966), p. 153.
3. *Ibid.*, p. 157. See also the delightfully ironic "I hasten to complete my list before I am interrupted" (*ibid.*, p. 35), which provides a refreshing pause in Nabokov's vivid but greatly detailed explanation of his "colored hearing."
4. Vladimir Nabokov, *Laughter in the Dark* (New York, 1961), p. 5.
5. *Ibid.*, p. 159.
6. Vladimir Nabokov, *Invitation to a Beheading* (New York, 1965), p. 223.

7. Vladimir Nabokov, *The Real Life of Sebastian Knight* (Norfolk, Conn., 1959), p. 205.
8. Vladimir Nabokov, *Despair* (New York, 1966), p. 174.
9. Nabokov, *Laughter in the Dark,* p. 113.
10. *Ibid.,* p. 158.
11. See also *ibid.,* pp. 146, 154, 159-60.
12. *Ibid.,* p. 35.
13. Vladimir Nabokov, *King, Queen, Knave* (New York, 1968), p. 64.
14. Nabokov, *Lolita,* p. 53.
15. *Ibid.,* p. 62.
16. Vladimir Nabokov, *Nikolai Gogol* (New York, 1944), pp. 1, 150.
17. Vladimir Nabokov, *Pnin* (New York, 1965), p. 174.
18. Nabokov, *Speak, Memory,* p. 139.
19. Nabokov, *Lolita,* p. 15.
20. *Ibid.,* p. 51.
21. Dabney Stuart, *"Laughter in the Dark:* Dimensions of Parody," *TriQuarterly* (Winter, 1970), pp. 76-7.
22. Nabokov, *Despair,* p. 28.
23. *Ibid.,* p. 151.
24. *Ibid.,* p. 21.
25. *Ibid.,* p. 173.
26. *Ibid.,* p. 17.
27. *Ibid.,* p. 27.
28. *Ibid.,* p. 161.
29. Nabokov, *King, Queen, Knave,* p. 8. My italics.
30. See, for example, *ibid.,* pp. 36, 103, 116.
31. See Vladimir Nabokov, *The Defense* (New York, 1964), pp. 76, 83; 39, 45, 135.
32. Nabokov, *Pale Fire,* p. 7.
33. *Ibid.,* p. 8.
34. *Ibid.,* p. 167.
35. *Ibid.,* p. 18.
36. Vladimir Nabokov, "The Potato-Elf," *The Single Voice,* Jerome Charyn, ed. (London, 1969), p. 61.
37. See Nabokov, *King, Queen, Knave,* pp. 102, 133. See also p. 271.
38. Nabokov, "The Potato-Elf," p. 59.
39. *Ibid.,* p. 72.
40. *Ibid.,* p. 61.
41. *Ibid.,* p. 73.
42. *Ibid.,* p. 75.
43. *Ibid.,* p. 57.
44. *Ibid.,* p. 63.
45. *Ibid.,* p. 71.
46. *Ibid.,* p. 60.
47. *Ibid.,* pp. 62, 65.
48. Nabokov, *Lolita,* p. 235. My italics.
49. *Ibid.,* p. 39.
50. *Ibid.,* p. 89.
51. *Ibid.,* p. 90.

52. *Ibid.*, p. 154. My italics.
53. *Ibid.*, p. 110.
54. *Ibid.*, p. 190.
55. *Ibid.*, p. 241.
56. *Ibid.*, p. 256.
57. *Ibid.*, p. 243.
58. *Ibid.*, p. 267.
59. *Ibid.*, p. 275.
60. *Ibid.*, p. 255.
61. *Ibid.*, p. 245.
62. *Ibid.*, p. 245.
63. *Ibid.*, p. 267.
64. Nabokov, *Despair*, p. 67. Nabokov often associates telephones with a character's thoughts and emotions. The telephone is usually personified and evokes a revealing reaction. Two examples:

> The ringing went on and on, with brief pauses to catch its breath. It did not wish to die; it had to be killed.

> (*The Gift*, New York, 1963, p. 178)

> . . . the telephone placed a cold hand on his shoulder.

> (*King, Queen, Knave*, p. 264)

The "hydrodynamic telephones" in *Ada* (p. 23) offer an interesting variation in sound that can be seen to echo in divers ways the significance of water in this novel. V., the narrator of *The Real Life of Sebastian Knight*, says: "I dislike telephoning." (p. 142)
In addition to the three instances discussed above, consider especially the following functions of telephones in Nabokov: *Ada*, pp. 13, 16, 260, 491; *The Defense*, pp. 37, 215, 231, 236; *Laughter in the Dark*, pp. 40, 41, 66, 93 155; *Nabokov's Dozen*, pp. 92, 106; *The Waltz Invention* (New York, 1966), p. 21; *King, Queen, Knave*, pp. 33, 91; *Pnin*, pp. 30-1, 189; *Bend Sinister* (London, 1960), p. 130; *The Gift*, pp. 97, 162, 396; *Lolita*, p. 58.
As seen above, alarm clocks, door bells, and so on function similarly though not as often. A further example: ". . . the door bell brutally rang." (*Nabokov's Quartet*, New York, 1966, p. 33)
65. Nabokov, *Despair*, p. 84.
66. *Ibid.*, p. 173.
67. *Ibid.*, p. 192.
68. Nabokov, *Lolita*, p. 222.
Van Veen's exasperation is constantly conveyed through the use of "idiotic" in otherwise quite objective narration. See, for example, Nabokov, *Ada*, pp. 145, 169, 200, 213, 385, and especially 393, 444, 514.
69. Nabokov, *Lolita*, p. 204.
70. *Nabokov's Dozen*, p. 49.
71. *Ibid.*, p. 50. My italics.
72. Further symptoms include the following:

Some of the spies are detached observers, such are [*sic*] glass surfaces and still pools; others, such as coats in store windows, are
prejudiced witnesses, lynchers at heart. . . .

(*Ibid.*, p. 50)

"Detached" functions as a gruesome pun indeed (his mirror-like
reflections are "separate" but hardly "objective" in their imputed
views). And the fact that the patient's own reflections are his enemies
seems a most appropriate irony. Note also the eerie, Gogolian impos-
sibility "at heart"—plus the fact that these coats, besides being
heart*less*, are in a very real sense "lynched" themselves, which ironically underlines their alleged intentions.

73. Andrew Field, *Nabokov: His Life in Art* (Boston, Mass., 1967), p. 180.
74. Nabokov, *The Defense*, p. 126. My italics.
75. *Ibid.*, p. 240.
76. Nabokov, *Pnin*, p. 23. My italics.
77. Nabokov, *Pale Fire*, p. 204.
78. Nabokov, *Laughter in the Dark*, pp. 78-9.
79. *Ibid.*, p. 37.
80. *Ibid.*, p. 91.
81. *Ibid.*, pp. 44-5.
82. *Ibid.*, p. 55.
83. *Ibid.*, pp. 146-7.
    Other *Laughter* syllogisms can be found in the "gloomy" birth
    of Elizabeth's daughter (p. 11), the auto accident (pp. 128-9: Albinus'
    dim vision, then special dexterity, leading to disaster), and even
    Margot's misleading, though ironically prophetic "voice break-off"
    when blind Albinus finally traps her in their former flat (p. 157).
84. *Ibid.*, p. 116.
85. *Ibid.*, p. 121.
86. Nabokov, *Ada*, p. 232.
87. Nabokov, *King, Queen, Knave*, p. 117.
88. Nabokov, *Lolita*, p. 105.
89. Nabokov, *Pale Fire*, p. 16.
90. Nabokov, *Lolita*, p. 244. See also the similar one-sentence "dramatic
    letter" syllogism, *Nabokov's Dozen*, p. 105. See also *Despair*, pp. 98-9.
91. *Ibid.*, pp. 117-8.
92. *Ibid.*, p. 134; amusingly introduced, p. 133.
93. Carl R. Proffer, *Keys To Lolita* (Bloomington, Indiana, 1968); see
    Chapter One and especially p. 52.
94. Nabokov, *Speak, Memory*, p. 21.
95. *Ibid.*, p. 275.
96. "Vladimir Nabokov Talks About Nabokov," *Vogue* (December, 1969),
    p. 190.
97. Field, p. 94.
98. Nabokov, *Nikolai Gogol*, p. 150.

*Part III*
*Sexual*
*Manipulations*

# 6.

*Austen*

*and Byron*

Typically, two of Nabokov's literary techniques effecting sexual deception are best explained in his own demonstration. Commenting on a pun by Pushkin (in a footnote to his *Eugene Onegin*), Nabokov has casually claimed:

> . . . the *double entente* of "modest" has escaped the notice of scholars, thus sharing the fate of the naval obscenity that Jane Austen, not understanding its full implications, allows Miss Crawford to repeat (presumably, after Charles Austen) in *Mansfield Park,* vol. I, ch. 6; and of the disgusting sustained pun running through a whole line in the last stanza of the much less innocent Lord Byron's *Beppo.*[1]

The line from *Beppo* reads: "My pen is at the bottom of a page," the three nouns of which serve as rather obvious puns.

The Austen "naval obscenity" occurs when Miss Crawford says:

> "Certainly, my home at my uncle's brought me acquainted with a circle of admirals. Of *Rears* and *Vices,* I saw enough. Now do not be suspecting me of a pun, I entreat."

Obviously, both *rears* and *vices* are puns, and one can easily imagine Miss Crawford's coy, demure smile. But as Eric Partridge has illustrated in Shakespeare, the word *vice* can mean "pudend and closed thighs," [2] a further pun of which Jane Austen was presumably unaware. And yet such a meaning, in conjunction with "rears," seems almost delightfully—if darkly—symmetrical. Here then, as is so often the case with Nabokov, the ultimate joke is on the smug deceiver. *Vices,* moreover, has three possible meanings; in the Russian version of *Lolita,* as shown below, a strikingly similar sexual pun has four. And in *Ada,* a French word used euphemistically for sexual intercourse *(ébats)* is actually in Russian a crude four-letter designation of the very same activity. [3]

Nabokov's own writings dimly glitter with deceptions of the two types cited above, yet critics have thus far accorded them surprisingly little attention. Here, discussion is confined primarily to the well-known *Lolita.* It seems convenient to treat first the Austen type (smug deceiver subtly deceived) and then the Byron variety (hidden sustained sexual metaphor). We should remember however that if intended at all, both types are presumably designed, in Nabokov's own phrase, to escape the notice of scholars.

Lolita's letter home from camp ("Dear Mummy and Hummy") contains the following:

> I [crossed out and re-written again] I lost my new sweater in the woods. [4] [Nabokov's brackets.]

Then, 98 pages later, Humbert thinks he hears Lolita's friend Mona joke about Lo's virgin wool sweater: "The only thing about you that is, kiddo. . . ." Since we have in the meantime learned of Lolita's losing her virginity to Charlie in the woods at camp, the meaning of her "new sweater" seems clear. Such retroactive revelations occur frequently in Nabokov.

But why was Lolita's "I" described as crossed out and then "re-written again"? Humbert is seldom idly redundant. And why, we might inquire, is the simple *I* so emphasized? The fact that Nabokov often punnishly plays with sounds, syllables and spellings seems to justify looking elsewhere in *Lolita*. At one place on the trail of a double deception (Hum and Lo fooling most of America; Lo fooling Hum), Lolita passes off Quilty as a woman, and Humbert asks:

> "So she complimented you?"
> "Complimented my eye—she kissed me on my pure brow"—and my darling emitted that new yelp of merriment which—perhaps in connection with her theatrical mannerisms—she had lately begun to affect.[5]

Here, much of the irony derives from "observant" Humbert's terming Lolita "my darling" just when she cryptographically speaks of being someone else's. Moreover, a slight alteration leads to Humbert's unwitting explanation: "in connection with her theatrical man." Such punnish possibilities are typical.[6]

But what if one places the fluff of Lo's virginal "brow" considerably lower? The phrase "complimented my eye" then becomes a masterpiece of extended pun ("complemented") plus extended sexual metaphor. (Eric Partridge offers the following explanation of Shakespeare's use of *eye* as a female sexual symbol: *"eye* because of the shape, the garniture of hair, and the tendency of both organs to become suffused with moisture." [7]) And, though both spellings of *complimented* work surpassing well in the sexual sense, the "i" in context can be deemed a hidden key to the sexual reading of "eye."

Especially ironic here is that Humbert is blind to this connotation of Lolita's eye, even while only the most agile reader pictures Quilty extending his complements. Nor does Lo's joke necessarily suggest that she is attuned to the full play of meaning her own words set to motion.

It is tempting, in light of this, to return to the Pushkin pun that interested Nabokov. Describing *"belles inaccessible"* in *Eugene Onegin*, Pushkin had written:

> above their eyebrows Hell's inscription: "Abandon hope for evermore!" [8]

Pushkin's own footnote to this explains he was "modest" enough to omit Dante's next phrase: "ye who enter here." [9] Thus it seems possible that both Pushkin and Nabokov had more in mind concerning the word *eyebrows* than their comments reveal.

In Nabokov's Russian version of *Lolita*, the "eye" colloquialism is missing, yet its potential implications fully remain. Lolita's answer becomes: ". . . kissed me on my little brow—on my pure little brow." (. . . *lobyznula v lobik—v moi chistyi lobik*.[10]) The word *lobik* (diminutive of *lob*, "brow,"—if the already infamous letter *i* is but changed to an *o*—becomes *lobok*, "the pubes." Also, the same root *(lob)* suggestively connects the verb *kissed* and *little brow*.

As we might expect from Nabokov, a subsequent reference to Lolita's "eye" is similarly suggestive. Humbert describes himself driving with Lolita, their car hotly followed by Quilty:

> And all the time I was aware of a private blaze on my right: her joyful eye, her flaming cheek.[11]

Both *private* and *cheek* serve as supporting puns for the "sexual eye" symbolism. Even *joyful* may be read: "full of amorous pleasure; full of pleasure in sexual intimacy." [12] Typically, Nabokov has Humbert sustain the joke upon himself, a deception which is ironically highlighted by "was aware of." And even the "private blaze" is echoed: Two pages later Humbert "teases" Lolita by pretending he thinks Quilty is "an ancient flame" of hers.

Two other potential *eye-I* echoes may be found on the page immediately following the "complimented" passage. First, Humbert says they crossed "the three states beginning with '*I* '"; then, he warns the reader that his narration is "not one of those honest mystery stories where all you have to do is keep an eye on the clues." Finally, an echo can even be seen in Lolita's refusing to describe Quilty's "weird, filthy, fancy" perversions:

> "Oh, I—really I"—she uttered the "I" as a subdued cry while she listened to the source of the ache. . . .[13]

Humbert himself employs a similar Austen-like pun when he has Lolita "locked in" their bedroom (and presumably drugged) on the eve of their first sleeping together. Gloatingly, he fondles his key "with its dangler of carved wood . . . the weighty sesame to a rapturous and formidable future." [14] Soon, after a reference to "neo-Freudian hash," Humbert gloats again: ". . . . the key was in my fist, my first was in my pocket, she was mine."

Thus, the reader feels smugly *au courant* as he reaches the end of this very Nabokovian passage:

> Naked, except for one sock and her charm bracelet, spread-eagled on the bed where my philter had felled her—so I foreglimpsed her . . . her honey-brown body . . . presented to me its pale breastbuds; in the rosy lamplight, a little pubic floss glistened on its plump hillock. The cold key with its warm wooden addendum was in my pocket.[15]

Diverted by Humbert's ironic jab at Freud, above, and luminous sensual detail, the smiling reader can easily fail to notice—despite its immediate proximity to *cold key*—the *lock* in *hillock*.

In Shakespeare, Partridge finds *lock* can mean "pudend" and "pick the lock"—"to force a woman's chastity." [16] Since Humbert still believes Lolita to be a virgin, his presumably unwitting pun can be seen to have ironic connotations.

One would hardly expect this intricate word play to be sustained in Nabokov's Russian version of *Lolita*. Yet it is. First, the word *klyuch* in Russian not only means "key" (both literally and figuratively) but also "source" or "spring" (in the sense of "origin" and "gushing water")—so the pun is at once fourfold! Moreover, "warm wooden addendum" becomes a punnish "dark (-skinned) nut (-wood) suspension" (*smuglym orekhovym priveskom*).[17] And, last but hardly least, the phrase "in my pocket" is in Russian only one vowel removed from "in my Carmen." As Carl Proffer has noted, Humbert often calls Lolita "Carmen." [18]

The lock-key theme echoes and re-echoes. Long before the bedroom episode, when Charlotte discovers Humbert's sordid little diary, he "surveys" his "raped little table with its open drawer, a key hanging from the lock." [19]

Later Humbert casually remarks: "I really did not mind where to dwell provided I could lock my Lolita up somewhere. . . ." [20] Although "somewhere" is presumably not a conscious pun, it is echoed still later, when Humbert informs Lolita, ostensibly referring to her suspicious absences: "I am ready to yank you out of Beardsley and lock you up you know where, but this must stop." [21] Not only does the double meaning survive independent of either Humbert's or Lolita's awareness, Nabokov has even provided an Aesopian apology for the pun-sated reader: "but this must stop." (The "where" is supposedly an old Appalachian farmhouse.) But stop it does not. About to kill Quilty, Humbert remarks:

> The house being an old one, had more planned privacy than have our modern glamour-boxes, where the bathroom, the only lockable locus, has to be used for the furtive needs of planned parenthood.[22]

Smiling at his own vivid vision, Humbert may well be entirely unaware of his long-sustained sexual pun "lockable."

Unwitting sexual puns of the Austen type are hardly confined to *Lolita*. In *King, Queen, Knave,* Franz observes his uncle's wife Martha, with whom he is soon to sleep:

> . . . a little dark down, the sign of passion, glistened above her upper lip, and a gleam of sun brought out the creamy texture of her neck at the throat as if traced with a fingernail across it, one above the other: *also* a token of all kinds of marvels according to one of his schoolmates, a precocious expert.[23]

"Also" is the key word here. The reader needs no great imagination, especially with the aid of that knowledgeable schoolmate, to construe the vague, "creamy" V at Martha's throat as a token of marvels below. The phrase "one above the other," then, becomes signally ambiguous (one line, or one V?). What tends to slip past unobserved, however, is that *also* (which speciously refers to "sign of passion," which in turn refers to Martha's very faint mustache) carries with it the "token of marvels" idea. Thus, the "little dark down" that "glistened above her upper lip" is a further potential reference to "down below," although only the "also" sends even the careful reader mentally back to see.

Martha's lips are continually mentioned at potentially "token" places throughout the novel.[24] One such instance describes her accompanying Franz as he goes to look for an apartment *before* their affair has begun.

> Franz exulted. What luck! . . . how splendid it was to stroll along with this red-lipped beauty . . . Add a new suit and a flaming tie—and his happiness would be complete.[25]

Nabokov is a master of the seemingly insignificant, yet subtly prophetic, detail. And this little passage is versatile indeed. Any reader in tune with Martha's "lips" will probably recognize their mention as the potential lovers go off together, alone, in potential search of a potential place to make love. But both Franz and the reader, who is thus drawn into his jubilant stream-of-consciousness, can easily fail to see that "new suit" readily construes as the prophylactic Martha is soon to dress him in—which dressing is of course followed by a "flaming tie" (both puns). But more: the word *happiness* is *later* defined, with derivative retroactive significance, as love play and sexual intercourse.

Once the affair is under way, we are told that Franz's department store job "prepared his hands for other motions and contact,"

> also rapid and nimble, causing Martha to purr with pleasure, for she particularly loved his forelimbs, and loved them most of all when with a succession of rhapsodic touches they would run all over her milk-white body. Thus a shop counter was the mute keyboard on which Franz had rehearsed his *happiness*.[26]

Carefully introduced by *rhapsodic,* the final image seems to parody

Shakespeare's Sonnet 128. The obvious ambiguity of *forelimbs* is yet richer because Franz's "index" (finger) has been already developed as his own "token" of a "marvel below." [27]

Martha's husband later reinforces the sexual definition of "happiness." Musing that Martha's "whole charm" may well lie "in the fact that she is so cold," he adds: "After all, there's a cold shiver in the sensation of true happiness." [28] Thus, the very Nabokovian "flaming tie" passage becomes completely clear only upon a close *re-reading* of the novel—unless, it seems one possesses a photographic memory or highly agile recall. But most important, Franz has no reason to be aware of his own extended prophetic metaphor ("new suit" . . . "flaming tie" . . . "complete happiness").

Early in *Lolita,* Humbert gleefully devises an extended sexual metaphor of the Byron type. But Nabokov, just off stage, gives his narrator's words an unwitting Austen twist. No sooner has Humbert, his lap alive with Lo, released some presumably unobserved ecstasy into his "royal robes" than he proceeds to boast as follows:

> The conjurer had poured milk, molasses, foaming champagne into a young lady's new purse; and lo, the purse was intact.[29]

As Proffer has noted, " 'Lo' and 'purse' are puns," [30] but more can be said. The trio of spermlike liquids are euphonically bound by a series of euphoric *m*'s. "Milk, molasses, foaming champagne" dismantles phonetically as m—mo—oam—m. Liquid *l*'s link *milk* with *molasses,* and a subtle sibilance unites *molasses* with *champagne.* Finally, the *o* of "mo—oam" very much becomes the *o* in *lo.* This "mo—oam" (almost a moan) is typical of the way Nabokov uses sound to round out his meaning.

Especially to be noted here is the grotesque definition of Lo—if *purse* is considered an appositive. Actually, *lo* reads sexually both as "Lo" and "low." Nor should *intact* slip by unnoticed, with its submeaning of "having the hymen unbroken; virginal," for then the laugh is ultimately on the clever deceiver. Humbert may well be pleased with his pun-filled description of his fun-filled deception, but his words are nonetheless ironic since he will later [31] wrongly suppose that Lo's "purse" is still "intact."

Finally, this little passage connects two of the novel's dominant sexual motifs: rising, bubbling "wine and its analogies" and Humbert as a money fountain for Lolita's purse. Not un-ironically, Nabokov has found it "a little painful" to "harp" on the former image,[32] yet his Humbert does so with considerably successful suggestiveness.[33] Nabokov's development of the latter theme [34] humorously includes some insinuations that Humbert frequently bribed Lolita with coins to comply with his more unsavory aspirations:

> Knowing the magic and might of her own soft mouth, she managed—during one school year!—to raise the bonus price of a fancy embrace to three, and even four bucks, O Reader! Laugh not, as you imagine me, on the very rack of joy emitting dimes and quarters . . .[35]

These "dimes and quarters" seem most appropriate, in type if not in timing, to the sexual "purse" metaphor.

Humbert's famous "cryptogrammic paper chase" [36] includes:

> "Lucas Picador, Merrymay, Pa.," insinuated that my Carmen had betrayed my pathetic endearments to the imposter.[37]

Proffer ably demonstrates that "Lucas" is Quilty—"In Prosper Merimée's story, *Carmen*, the heroine leaves her lover for a picador named Lucas. . . ." [38] But why does Humbert find his "pathetic endearments" here "betrayed"? "Picador" surely construes as a sexual pun (not unlike the ones in *Beppo*),[39] supported later by the "crazy things, filthy things" Lolita admits Quilty wanted her to do—things that Humbert renders by the French *"souffler."* [40] And what of Humbert himself? In addition to the "fancy embrace" presumably exploiting "the might and magic of her soft mouth," Lolita is further described by Humbert as "preparing her homework, sucking a pencil." [41] These two phrases seem suspiciously close. In fact, this apparently casual juxtaposition may well be a typical trap for the "eager Freudian sleuth," who, perhaps missing its appositional possibilites entirely, smugly smiles at the echo of Lolita's "gnawing a pencil" earlier, at school, with "all the boys' eyes on her hair and neck." [42] If "homework," above, is construed sexually, the amusingly sex-preoccupied Miss Pratt's observation becomes doubly ironic: "She has no regular home duties, I understand." [43]

Given Nabokov's interest in sexual meanings which can be seen to lurk behind classical literary lines, it seems not impossible that he concludes his *Eugene Onegin* Commentary with a muffled, sustained burst of sexual fun. (If so, Nabokov will thus be seen to echo, in both timing and type of *double entendre,* his own example taken from Byron's *Beppo.*[44])

In approaching the passage below, one should note that although the concept of "masculine and feminine rhyme" offers rich cryptographic potential, there are absolutely no provable clues. Even the words *masculine* and *feminine* seem quite naturally employed. Hence, we are now entering a highly improbable realm, but perhaps a strangely possible one in terms of Nabokov's natural habit of thought.

> The reader should be careful not to confuse the scudded masculine rhyme with the long rhyme. In the following example, all six lines are in iambic tetrameter, with a long rhyme in 1 and 3, a masculine rhyme in 2 and 4, and a feminine rhyme with a contraction in 5 and 6.

> The man who wants to write a triolet,
> When choosing rhymes should not forget
> That some prefer a triple violet
> And some a single violet;
> Nor should he spurn the feminine vi'let
> Blooming, contracted, on its islet.[45]

If, for discussion of this triolet presumably concocted by Nabokov, *masculine* and *feminine* are taken secondarily in the sexual sense, it seems not inappropriate to construe *rhyme,* with its goallike quality of terminal harmony, as the sexual climax. (There are possibly two tiny clues in this regard—1016 pages earlier—when

Nabokov speaks of Pushkin's "unexpected mating by rhyme," plus "the acrobatic brilliance of the Russian rhyme." [46]) And, having taken *rhyme* as *climax,* one is hard put to deny that the "scudded masculine rhyme" is indeed different in nature from the "long [feminine] rhyme." Note also Nabokov's humorous warning lest the reader "confuse" the two. Moreover, the "contracted feminine vi'let" (which "the man" should not spurn) construes very vividly in the sexual sense, especially when "blooming on its islet." [47]

*Violet* takes little alteration to produce *violate,* which fits rather graphically into the sexual, or rhyme, scheme. *Choosing rhymes,* then, assumes not a few improper little hues, especially in conjunction with the *triple* violet [48] that "some prefer." (The parallel with *Beppo* continues.)

*Islet,* however, waxes richest of all. Besides "little island" and, phonetically, "I let," it can easily be read "little eye"—a striking echo of Lolita's *eye,* above.

Given *rhyme* as climax, *line*—with its calculated rhythmical development—can be construed as a single sexual act. *Metrical scheme,* as a sort of regulated tempo, finds its place as well. Nabokov's next sentence (which begins his last paragraph) is:

> The fact that rhyme, no matter its length, lies outside the metrical scheme of the line leads to some droll results.

Droll indeed. If "lies outside" means "does not fit into the pattern of," then, not unhumorously, the rhyme, or climax, comes to mean a rather unmetrical, uncontrolled culmination. And, if *lies* is taken as *seems false,* the humor is but increased: despite all efforts to be true to the "metrical scheme," this somehow proved impossible. *Outside* is also susceptible to triple interpretation. Besides both musical and locational constructions with respect to "(masculine and feminine) rhyme," it can even be seen to hint at the Nabokovian *leitmotiv* of homosexuality and/or perversion: "The fact that a climax, no matter how long, is false outside of normal intercourse leads to some droll results."

"If we devise, for example," Nabokov goes on,

an iambic couplet in which the rhyme is not merely long, but monstrous and, indeed, a very sea serpent in length, we shall see that despite there being six additional syllables after the ictus, making fourteen syllables in all of the line, the latter still remains a tetrameter (or "octosyllable," as some would call it):

> *Est' rífmï próchnie, napráshivayushchiesya,*
> *I mnogonózhki ést', podkáshivayushchiesya*

which means in prose, "There are solid rhymes that suggest themselves readily, and centipedes, whose legs buckle under them."

The potential play on *couplet,* and on *long and monstrous rhyme,* should be obvious. Also subject to sexual interpretation are the "solid rhymes that suggest themselves readily," as well as the writhing rhyme, or climax, that a simple substitution will produce. *Ictus,* in addition to "metrical stress or beat," can mean "a pulsation" or "a fit."

With almost diabolical unlikeliness, the potential extended metaphor carries consistently on to the very end:

This couplet is identical in metrical length with, say:

> *Est' rífmï tóchnie, i ést'*
> *Drugie. Vséh ne perechést'*

which means, "There are exact rhymes, and there are other ones. All cannot be listed."

Finally, almost as if in belated corroboration of the above improbabilities, Van Veen mentions

> ". . . a snatch of Pushkin, for the sake of rhyme—"
> "For the *snake* of rhyme!" cried Ada.[49]

And here the word *snatch* can be seen to inter-echo with the

pun in Ada's earlier statement about Van's shattal-tree kiss:
". . . a time when the chastest of chances allowed you to snatch,
as they say, a first shy kiss!" [50] Note also the typical Aesopean
apology: "as they say."

## Notes

1. Vladimir Nabokov, *Eugene Onegin* (New York, 1964), vol. II, p. 368.
2. Eric Partridge, *Shakespeare's Bawdy* (New York, 1969), p. 212.
3. Vladimir Nabokov, *Ada* (New York, 1969), p. 395. More than one
   critic has enjoyed discovering the bilingual pun in Mona's letter to
   Lolita:

   > *il faut qu'il t'y mène.* Lucky beau! *Qu'il t'y*—What a tongue-
   > twister! Well, be good, Lollikins.

   [Vladimir Nabokov, *Lolita* (New York, 1959), p. 204]

   But Nabokov seldom reveals his deceptions so easily. And, given
   Quilty's interest in fellatio (see p. 252), "tongue-twister" functions as
   a vivid and vulgar pun indeed. "The letter," Nabokov has Humbert
   tell us, "contained an element of mysterious nastiness that I am too
   tired to-day to analyze." Note also the ironic juxtaposition of "tongue-
   twister" and "Well, be good." Even "*Lolli*kins" may be read suggestively; and two pages later Lolita tells Humbert: "Okay, so we
   did not have a pop." (Fooling him as usual, she is apparently unaware
   of her own potential sexual pun.)
   Nabokov is ingeniously sensitive to meanings suggested by parts
   of words: "beautiful word, stratogem—a treasure in a cave." [*Nikolai
   Gogol* (New York, 1944), p. 59.] In *Despair* (New York, 1966, p. 199)
   he has devised for Hermann a bilingual word-part pun of the Austen
   type described above. Smugly mentioning "Rascalnikov" (an obvious
   play on "rascal" and Dostoevsky's "Raskolnikov," hero of *Crime and
   Punishment*)—Hermann may well be unaware that the (stressed)
   syllable he has created, *cal,* is phonetically identical to the Russian
   word *kal, excrement.*
4. Nabokov, *Lolita*, p. 76.
5. *Ibid.,* p. 191.
6. For example: ". . . her bicycle manner, I mean her approach to it,
   the hip movement in mounting . . ." (*Ibid.,* p. 182).
7. Partridge, p. 102.
   By a striking and probably purposeful coincidence, Van speaks
   of paying Ada eight "compliments" (*Ada,* p. 196), which cryptographically signifies eight sexual climaxes.
8. Nabokov, *Eugene Onegin*, Vol. I, p. 164.
9. *Ibid.,* p. 326.
10. Vladimir Nabokov, *Lolita* [in Russian] (New York, 1967), p. 190.

11. Nabokov, *Lolita*, p. 200.
12. See Partridge, p. 128.
13. Nabokov, *Lolita*, p. 22. See also ". . . the flesh and the eye you alone are elected to know . . . *Ibid.*, p. 50, and Appendix F.
14. *Ibid.*, p. 114.
15. *Ibid.*, p. 115.
16. Partridge, pp. 139, 159, respectively.
17. Nabokov, *Lolita* [in Russian], p. 111.
18. Carl R. Proffer, *Keys To Lolita* (Bloomington, Indiana, 1968), p. 16.
    In the Russian *Lolita*, this punnish combination ("in my pocket" —"in my Carmen") is carefully prefigured by the translation of "Dwarf Conductors" (Humbert's name for Lolita's favorite phonograph record, p. 44) as *"Karmannaya Karmen"* ("Pocket Carmen," p. 35; echoed, p. 49)—which almost suggests that Nabokov was thinking at least partially and presciently in Russian when he composed the English *Lolita*.
19. Nabokov, *Lolita*, p. 89.
20. *Ibid.*, p. 161.
21. *Ibid.*, p. 187.
22. *Ibid.*, p. 268.
23. Vladimir Nabokov, *King, Queen, Knave* (New York, 1968), p. 6. My italics.
24. See, in addition to the passage discussed below, *ibid.*, pp. 14, 17, 49, 59, 62, 102, 129, and especially the long "cold chicken bone" Freud spoof, p. 123.
25. *Ibid.*, p. 51.
26. *Ibid.*, p. 104. My italics.
27. See *ibid.*, p. 28 for "index" (echoed, pp. 42, 63) and p. 103 for appreciation of "marvel below."
28. *Ibid.*, p. 176.
29. Nabokov, *Lolita*, p. 59.
30. Proffer, p. 153.
31. See Nabokov, *Lolita*, p. 114.
32. See *Eugene Onegin*, vol. III, p. 298.
33. See Nabokov, *Lolita*, pp. 7, 17, 19, 20-1, 50, 55, 57, 73, and especially 124, 144-5, 189, 206, 264.
34. See *ibid.*, pp. 107, 112, 127.
35. *Ibid.*, p. 168.
36. *Ibid.*, p. 228.
37. *Ibid.*, p. 229.
38. Proffer, p. 16.
39. In Philip Roth's *Portnoy's Complaint*, which Nabokov has summarily disparaged [*The New York Times* (April 19, 1969), p. 20.], one can find: ". . . pick a hole, any hole, I'm yours!" (New York, 1969, p. 196), Nabokov's version does seem somewhat more subtle.
40. Nabokov, *Lolita*, p. 252.
41. *Ibid.*, p. 175.
42. *Ibid.*, p. 51.
43. *Ibid.*, p. 178.

44. As stated earlier, the line reads: "My pen is at the bottom of a page." A veiled allusion thereto may be found in *Pale Fire* when Kinbote depicts the aftermath of the Zemblan Revolution. "The bedrooms of the few remaining palace attendants," he relates, "had each its armed parasite, drinking forbidden rum with an old footman or taking liberties with a young page." For the reader attuned to Byron, Kinbote's next sentence seems most ambiguous:

> And in the great Herald's Hall one could always be sure of finding ribald jokers trying to squeeze into the steel panoply of its hollow knights.

[Vladimir Nabokov, *Pale Fire* (New York, 1966), p. 86]

This may be totally innocent, but the possible sexual meaning of "trying to squeeze into" (supported by "ribald") can easily be seen to develop the "liberties taken with a young page" in the manner of Byron's veiled *Beppo* obscenity.

45. *Eugene Onegin,* Vol. III, pp. 539-40.

46. *Ibid.,* Vol. II, p. 71.

47. "A well-known contraction is 'flower,'" Nabokov earlier remarks (*ibid.,* Vol. III, p. 476) and proceeds to juxtapose: "maid'nhead," "vi'let." Discussion there also includes "such rhymes as hour-our (cf. higher-fire)"—an *almost* impossible echo of "your pillow has been creased/ By our two heads. . . . our common hour." (*Pale Fire,* lines 276-9)

48. See, in this regard, the "Picador" pun discussed above in *Lolita.*

49. Nabokov, *Ada,* p. 246.

50. *Ibid.,* p. 95.

# 7.

*Symbols
and Backgrounds*

In *Ada,* Morris Dickstein writes, Nabokov "has taken advantage of our new freedom of sexual description." [1] Actually, such freedom has long been deftly and artistically taken by Nabokov, but far less obviously. As a result, his many sexual symbols inter-echo self-enhancingly, from page to page, from book to book.

Often it seems that Nabokov composes with constant reference to Freud's famous lecture "Symbolism in Dreams"; the symbols therein are religiously punished. Frequent warnings about "cruel traps set for Freudians" deceptively tend to excuse the lack of subtlety in such thrusts and to imply that their suggestiveness is beneath Nabokov the serious artist. Humor provides further exoneration. And Nabokov adds his own little twists. According to Freud, for example, playing the piano in a dream indicates "gratification derived from a person's own genitals." [2] The "keyboard" passage in *King, Queen, Knave* apparently fits Franz's fingers to Martha, but Franz incorrigibly masturbates.[3] A Freudian slip by Martha[4] concerns "slippers"—a euphemism for her love making with Franz.[5] According to Freud, "slippers symbolize the female genital organs." [6]

Although Nabokov especially favors such obvious symbols as knobbed canes (sometimes even sucked),[7] his echoing sexual symbolism is ingeniously diverse. By echo, Ada seems fond of sucking her big toe; [8] Hermann *(Despair)* says his *(imaginary)* brother "could not go to sleep without sucking my big toe." [9]

During a dinner shared by two pairs of furtive lovers (Demon, Marina, Ada, Van), there is casual mention of ". . . the young lady's fare of *asperges en branches* that everybody was now enjoying.

> It almost awed one to see the pleasure with which she and Demon distorted their shiny-lipped mouths in exactly the same way to introduce orally from some heavenly height the voluptuous ally of the prim lily of the valley, holding the shaft with an identical bunching of the fingers. . . .[10]

So steeply sensual does this passage become that the redundant word "orally" [11] seems at once vaguely humorous and yet abruptly unpleasant. But puns, as usual, make for a humor which tends to mute repulsiveness. (*"En branches"* both punnishly and vividly suggests the reading: "every body was now enjoying.")

Especially as a "young lady's fare," the as-good-as-Freud-ordered asparagus [12] brings to life an entire night-blooming garden of metaphorical meaning. *Shaft,* of course, serves as a pun, as does the entire idea expressed by "the voluptuous ally of the prim lily of the valley." [13] Even *asperges* serves as a pun ("sprinkling with holy water"): its second meaning is then reflected in a "sign of the cross" finger-position comparison.

As dinner continues, we read that "Van remembered" someone who "used to say that the only vulgar passage" in Pushkin's work

> was the cannibal joy of young gourmets tearing "plump and live" oysters out of their "cloisters" in an unfinished canto of *Eugene Onegin.*" [14]

This is directly followed by the casual remark that "everyone has his own taste"—a "mistranslation" of *"chacun à son gout."* [15]

Such triple puns involving two languages are not uncommon in
*Ada.*

The oyster passage in Pushkin is an old favorite with Nabokov; he has focused upon it before—in his *Eugene Onegin*
Commentary.[16] The clue is worth tracing because it leads us,
with genial deviousness, back to the asparagus passage in *Ada.*
The Pushkin passage, in Nabokov's own translation, reads:

> What news of oysters? They have come. O glee!
> off flies gluttonous juventy
> to swallow from their sea shells
> the plump, live cloisterers,
> lightly asperged with lemon.[17]

*Asperged* thus rounds out another triple pun, this time in two
volumes and in a debatable number of languages.

In the 1968 English version of *King, Queen, Knave* Nabokov
employs some relatively obvious oyster symbolism:

> Because he wore glasses even for love-making, he reminded
> her of a handsome, hairy young pearl diver ready to pry the
> live pearl out of its rosy shell . . .[18]

Here the reader who hurries on in search of more explicit
maneuvers and manipulations will be disenchanted, but the
metaphor is ingeniously complete. Assonance typically enhances
vividness: *reminded, diver, pry, live pearl.*

*The Exploit* (in Russian, 1932) may be seen to contain a
more subtle, but similar instance. Martyn absent-mindedly muses
about the repulsiveness of pearls: "Oysters' hemorrhoids, roundish,
with an unhealthy sheen." [19] The Russian word *otblesk* ("sheen")
can also suggest "flow," "pouring off," or "low-tide." The very
next sentence (within the same paragraph) describes a street-
walker with whom Martyn immediately goes off and makes love.
(He begins even in the taxi.)

Nabokov's note to Pushkin's line "the plump, live cloisterers"
focuses in some detail upon the scene in *Anna Karenin* where

Oblonski vividly enjoys eating oysters.[20] In both Nabokov's Russian (1930) and English (1964) versions of *The Defense,* we read that Luzhin "like *Anna Karenin*—particularly the pages on the zemstvo elections and the dinner ordered by Oblonski.[21]

Such haunting echoes are typical of Nabokov's world, wherein time seems curiously destroyed and similar things forever seem to happen quite differently. Confronted by Clarence Brown's charge of repeating himself continually, Nabokov has characteristically transformed apparent weakness into apparent strength:

> Derivative writers seem versatile because they imitate many others. . . . Artistic originality has only its own self to copy.[22]

But the word *copy* misleadingly tends to isolate the components of Nabokov's uniquely rounded world of intricate, and self-enhancing, repetitions and echoes.

On Ada's twelfth birthday we learn that she is wont to affect, during the summer heat, an "omission of panties":

> The child tried to assuage the rash in the soft arch, with all its accompaniment of sticky, itchy, not altogether unpleasurable sensations, by tightly straddling the cool limb of a Shattal apple tree . . .[23]

The rather Dostoevskian usage of the word "child" perversely tends to draw our attention to the fact that Ada no longer is one. And in light of this implied precociousness, "the rash" seems a fitting potential pun. Extremely Nabokovian is the flow of stressed assonance ("assuage . . . unpleasurable sensations"), which tends to wash away the (also typically) resisting prefix "un." The unchild's pleasures thus seem stubbornly great.

Two chapters later we find Ada and Van "climbing the glossy-limbed shattal tree at the bottom of the garden."

> Van, in a blue gym suit, having worked his way up to a fork just under his agile playmate . . . betokened mute

communication by taking her ankle between finger and thumb as *she* would have a closed butterfly.[24]

"Butterfly," in Nabokov's works, can often be seen to symbolize the female private parts. Above, one has only to read the word *as* as *when* (or especially as *since*) to effect the transformation, which is carefully screened, but not at all encumbered, by the italics of *"she."*

> Her bare foot slipped, and the two panting youngsters tangled ignominiously among the branches . . . and the next moment . . . his expressionless face and cropped head were between her legs and a last fruit fell with a thud—the dropped dot of an inverted exclamation point.[25]

Given an "omission of panties," the words "panting" and "branches" construe quite vividly as improper puns. Most vivid of all, however, is Van's (very hidden) "expressionless face." And a Gogolian haunting return via an utterly disabled exclamation point highlights the irony.

At this juncture Ada and Van discuss the event in parentheses (a feature of the novel's sly-rich style, whereby the past is painted in the present), and she reminds-tells him-us: ". . . you kissed me here, on the inside—" [26] Even the past-present then suffers a slight displacement, as we read that

> . . . according to a later (considerably later!) version they were still in the tree, and still glowing, when Van removed a silk thread of larva web from his lip and remarked that such negligence of attire was a form of hysteria.[27]

The "silk thread of larva web" seems to echo "butterfly," above. Which association, en route, alights briefly upon "kissed me here," [28] as the phrase "negligence of attire" also serves to suggest and confirm.

Earlier in the novel, an excerpt from Ada's diary erotically describes the caterpillar of "the modest Puss Moth."

. . . with front segments shaped like bellows and a face resembling the lens of a folding camera. If you gently stroke its bloated smooth body, the sensation is quite silky and pleasant—until the irritated creature ungratefully squirts at you an acrid fluid from a slit in its throat.[29]

Watching an "enchanting" moth, Cincinnatus *(Invitation to a Beheading)*, "unable to restrain himself, stroked with his fingertip the hoary ridge near the base of the right wing, then the ridge of the left one (what gentle firmness, what unyielding gentleness! . . ." [30] Earlier, this moth is enthusiastically described at some length. The detail given includes: "Its segmented limbs, in fluffy muffs, now clung, now unstuck themselves. . . ." [31] Shade writes of his wife in "Pale Fire":

Come and be worshipped, come and be caressed,
My dark Vanessa, crimson-barred, my blest
My Admirable butterfly! [32]

Demon says that Ada and Lucette once drew his attention to a "tremendous garden of tongue-in-cheek delights" *(cheek* is a pun), "namely, to the butterflies in it." [33] He goes on to mention the "exact knowledge *on the part* of those two *admirable* little girls" and "the myth behind the moth." [34] And a Red Admirable butterfly appears "out of nowhere" at the end of Chapter Two in *King, Queen, Knave* (while Martha looms ever closer to seducing Franz) and begins "to fan" its wings "slowly as if breathing." Here however the symbolism seems rather far-fetched and only acquires suggestive connotations in the total context of Nabokov's world.

Watching Ada painting early in the novel, Van proceeds at length to "let his parched lips travel down her warm hair and hot nape" until he experiences a "despair of desire." And this situation touches off a persistent theme in Nabokov:

Silently he would slink away to his room, lock the door, grasp a towel, uncover himself, and call forth the image

he had just left behind, an image still as safe and bright as
a hand-cupped flame—carried into the dark, only to be got rid
of there with savage zeal; after which, drained for a while,
with shaky loins and weak calves, Van would return. . . .[35]

Narration subtly stresses the episode as habitual: "would slink
away . . . would return." "Himself" is a typical Nabokovian
sexual synecdoche. Less obvious is the fact that the image left
behind, when called forth, becomes both a mental and physical
one in the all-revealing darkness: "an image still as safe and
bright as a hand-cupped flame." Considering the close coopera-
tion here between mind and matter, such double symbolism
seems most appropriate. And the word *safe,* as a semi-pun, consistently supplements both images. Moreover, *safe* is linked to
*flame* by assonance, as is *bright* to the somewhat ironic "left
behind."

Two companion symbols—fireflies and candles [36]—intensify
and further develop the attraction of Ada's butterfly-moth to
Van's lone flame. Soon after his arrival at Ardis Hall, he asks her:

"By the way, do fireflies burn one if they fly into you? I'm
just asking. Just a city boy's silly question." [37]

Van later describes at length "the males of the firefly." He
speaks of them forming a "ghostly multitude" and mentions their
"quest" coming "to its natural end." Then, nocturnally athirst
for Ada, Van attempts to fall asleep:

. . . the fascinating fireflies, and the still more eerie pale
cosmos coming through the dark foliage, balanced with new
discomforts the nocturnal ordeal, the harassments of sweat
and sperm associated with his stuffy room.[38]

After "fly into you" and "burn," above, this combining of "sperm"
and "fascinating fireflies" seems quite suggestive.

Van's first climax with Ada herself (rather than her called-
forth image) occurs late at night while both "children," scantily

clothed, watch a "burning barn" from the window. Van, we are told, "relieved her of her candlestick, placing it near his own longer one on the window ledge." [39] The phrase "his own longer one" seems faintly, humorously ambiguous. And Ada immediately sustains the potential sexual meaning:

> "You are naked, you are dreadfully indecent," she observed without looking and without any emphasis or reproof, where-upon he cloaked himself tighter . . .

As usual, the allegedly denied is the vividly described: "observed without looking." The two then proceed to make puppy love, ever more strenuous:

> . . . one flame crepitated, one cushion was on the floor), "why do you get so fat and hard there when you—"

"One flame" seems quite obviously ambiguous.

Ada unskillfully but satisfactorily helps Van achieve a climax, whereupon he stretches himself naked in the "now motionless candlelight." She "presently" watches the "ponderous upswing of virile revival," and they now attempt intercourse, but Van prematurely bursts

> . . . at the lip of the orchid . . . *the firefly signals* were cir-cumscribing the reservoir. . . .[40]

Further developed by "circumscribing the reservoir," the "fire-fly signals" become more obviously symbolic. But very few readers will recall that eighteen pages before, during "our children's kissing phase," when their "raging bodies" somehow avoided intercourse, that "contacts and reactions to contacts could not help coming through like a distant vibration of desperate signals."

The candle-butterfly/moth theme finds a humorous echo late in the novel, in a letter written by Van to Ada:

. . . bed, around which you flutter, my Zegris butterfly, straightening a comically drooping candle . . .[41]

Nabokov's firefly and moth symbolism, though far more subtly, can be seen to function as early as *Bend Sinister* (written 1943-5). A long and *poshlust*-filled digression finally turns to the clandestine erotic pastimes of various "Mr. Etermons":

. . . a third Etermon with a fourth Etermon's wife anxiously discusses the future of a child she has managed to bear him in secret during the time her husband (now back in his arm-chair at home) was fighting in a remote jungle land where, *in his turn,* he has seen moths the size of a spread fan, and trees at night pulsating rhythmically with countless fireflies. No, the average vessels are not as simple as they appear: it is a conjuror's set and nobody, not even the enchanter him-self, really knows what and how much they hold.[42]

The passage can be seen, especially thanks to "in his turn," to describe symbolically the fourth Etermon's reciprocal unfaithful-ness. "Fighting" may seem a rather absurd euphemism for the sexual act, but humor sometimes conduces to unusual clarity. "Remote jungle land," "moths the size of a spread fan," and "trees pulsating with countless fireflies" all can be read sexually—especially in retrospect. Less obviously, "vessels," "the enchanter," and "what and how much they hold" can be seen to suggest seduction, adultery, and even the above "secret child." More generally, "conjuror's set" can be found to inter-echo with "the conjurer" who pours metaphorical sperm into Lolita's "purse," as well as "the conjurer," below, who fascinates Kinbote by mak-ing "his spoon dissolve" simply "by twiddling it." And thus, the metaphor here perhaps secretly suggests "the unseen symbolic capacity" of the preceding moth and firefly images, much as Nabokov's "revealing" his chess "symbols," below, seems poten-tially quite ironic.

Also in *Bend Sinister,* old Adam Krug is almost seduced by

the quite Lolita-like Mariette. (She has "chestnutty-smelling bare arms," a "peachblow silhouette," and we read that "Her pale young legs invited an old man's groping hand." [43]) "Shall we make love if I stay?" she asks, and, regarding her hips he remarks: "This is the pink moth clinging—" [44] Though they are interrupted at this point, the moth symbolism seems clear enough in retrospect. Incidentally, *Bend Sinister* ends with the sentence "A good night for mothing," the last word of which, Nabokov has insisted, is not a misprint.

When Pedro informs Ada that her "leetle aperture must be raccommodated" and places "a wet finger on the hole in her swimsuit," [45] these symbols seem almost painfully obvious. Humbert's "muscular thumb" that he envisions "reaching the hot hollow" of Lolita's groin,"[46] echoed later by hitchhikers "almost priapically thrusting out tense thumbs," [47] seems only slightly more subtle.

Somewhat similarly, Franz's "index" finger *(King, Queen, Knave)* seems sexually symbolic.[48] And, describing a secret Karlist hand signal, Kinbote writes:

> . . . the hand held in horizontal position with the index curved rather flaccidly and the rest of the fingers bunched (many have criticized it for looking too droopy; it has now been replaced by a more virile combination).[49]

In a homosexual's narration, the Nabokovian potential pun *index,* sustained by *droopy* and *virile,* seems doubly amusing. In view of this, it appears slightly curious that Kinbote has very little to say about the following six lines from "Pale Fire." Shade writes: "I pare/ My fingernails and vaguely am aware

> Of certain flinching likeness: the thumb,
> Our grocer's son; the index, lean and glum
> College astronomer Starover Blue;
> The middle fellow, a tall priest I knew;
> The feminine fourth finger, an old flirt;
> And little pinky clinking to her skirt." [50]

For the reader who envisions all this finger enumeration as homosexually symbolic, the last line comes as something of a shock: the "old flirt" becomes abruptly a genuine female. But until then each finger, as described, seems surprisingly appropriate to its owner in the sexual sense. As usual the potential pun "index" is present, and one almost suspects a "flinching" Kinbote of having altered the text—and then making a smooth and graceful exit. His only note to these lines, moreover, relates specifically to "Starover Blue" (the index), who, Kinbote seems to pun, "reminds one of the Royal Game of the Goose . . . a wild-goose game, rather. . . ." [51] This same note also refers the reader to Kinbote's "note to line 627," which explains the Russian pun *starover*—"Old Believer (member of a schismatic sect)." [52] The potential pun *member* of course reinforces *index*. And this second footnote is surprisingly suggestive of the "asparagus passage" in *Ada:*

> . . . holding the shaft with an identical bunching of the fingers, not unlike the reformed "sign of the cross" . . . (a ridiculous little schism measuring an inch or so from thumb to index). . . . [53]

And this may even re-echo with Kinbote's mention of "an asparagus dream." [54]

Not only is the astronomer, in the poem, humorously described (by potential sexual metaphor) as "lean and glum"; Kinbote adds, in his second note: "Honest Starover Blue will probably be surprised by the epithet bestowed upon him by a jesting Shade." [55] But why should *Shade* jest? If we remember Kinbote's "maddening and embarrassing experience at the college indoor swimming pool," [56] however, it seems clear that he could easily have had a most exact knowledge of the "glumly honest" astronomer's "lean index."

But could Kinbote, even seeking revenge for Zembla's absence, have altered Shade's poem? It is tempting to think so,[57] although the potential symbolism discussed here is typical of Nabokov and may have been "inserted" as a subtle joke upon an unwitting and innocent Shade.

In his commentary, Kinbote speaks of "the lust that Nature, the grand cheat, puts into us to inveigle us into propagations." [58] From a homosexual, this remark seems doubly disdainful. But *grand* survives as a humorous pun. In the poem "Pale Fire," there is an apparently casual aside about how man is "quick to recognize Natural shams, and then before his eyes"

> The reed becomes a bird, the knobby twig
> An inchworm, and the cobra head, a big
> Wickedly folded moth.[59]

These two and a half lines are laden with ripe sexual connotations. The reed, as it abruptly rises for flight, but sets the stage: given this startling upward motion, the male form of "knobby twig become inchworm" is vivid indeed and even seems to echo Nabokov's often-present "knobbed cane." The Nabokovian (female) "moth" is subtly enhanced by the shape of "cobra head." And *Wickedly* construes not only as a colloquial off-color pun of *wick,*—from Kinbote's, from the homosexual's point of view, the moth is, not unhumorously, wicked indeed.

Gardens of course symbolize, in Freud's view, the female genitalia.[60] *Ada* is a veritable garden of sensual, and erotically symbolic flowers. Ada herself says: *"My* flower opens only at dusk." [61] Cincinnatus "fiddles" with the "curled petal tips" of a "moist white rose." [62] Mac's "raw paw" melts *(Bend Sinister)* "because of" Mariette's "burning rose." [63] Humbert calls Lolita his "brown flower" and refers to her "brown rose." [64] Liza's poetry *(Pnin)* is said to contain "erotic undercurrents"; its translation reads:

> No jewels, save my eyes, do I own,
> but I have a rose which is even
> softer than my rosy lips.[65]

*Despair* contains numerous passages that seem to use the role of gardener as a euphemism, or sly symbol, for homosexual.[66] Kinbote constantly describes his own "gifted gardener" [67] with intense homosexual interest.[68]

The final (printed) lines of "Pale Fire" are:

> A man, *unheedful of the butterfly*—
> Some neightbor's gardener, I guess—goes by
> Trundling an empty barrow up the lane.[69]

In context of course the butterfly refers most obviously to a just-mentioned "dark Vanessa." But whether created by Nabokov or Kinbote, the (italicized) hidden fun here seems definitely at Shade's unwitting expense—especially since he has spoken of his own wife as the butterfly he carresses.[70] He even calls her "My dark Vanessa." [71]

Nabokov favors a very special type of narrator with a tendency to dramatize [72] and to color sexually his own narration. The resulting effect is a humorous, faintly elegant, and relentless sexual perception of "reality." And the telling method thus creates a sensual background that serves to highlight and intensify whatever sexual episodes and symbols are woven into the plot.

Hermann *(Despair)*, for example, speaks of "aphrodisiacally burbling" rain, "phallic tulips," the "virginity of pig leather" in suitcase shops, a hand extended (to be shaken) "as if it held a dirty postcard," a "miscarriage" in getting a visa, the "wind roughly upturning the several petticoats of the olive trees which it tumbled," and the "athletic torsos of the cork oaks." [73] He also notices, after first meeting the tramp Felix, "that pathetically impersonal trace which the unsophisticated wanderer is wont to leave under a bush: one large, straight, manly piece and a thinner one coiled over it." [74] The key word is *manly*—humorously incongruous but deftly dramatic. Hermann's attitude also hints at a most unusual definition of sophistication.

The homosexual Kinbote describes himself as "bent" under "the incubus of curiosity," refers to "our cynical age of frenzied heterosexualism," and mentions a "compact firearm in its case of suede leather hardly bigger than a castlegate key or a boy's seamed purse. . . ." [75] The sly symbolic possibilities of this last description are typical. Kinbote also tells of a "college porter who one day, in the Projection Room, showed a squeamish coed something of which she had no doubt seen better samples." [76] The key words of course are "no doubt." But the faint suggestiveness of a (capitalized) projection room also seems quite inspirational.

Kinbote elsewhere offers: "I have often felt when leaving a place that I have enjoyed, somewhat like a tight cork that is drawn out for the sweet dark wine to be drained, and then you are off to new vineyards and conquests." [77] He also constantly imputes sexual activities and inspirations to others. Gerald Emerald is blithely presumed to be conducting an "investigation of some mammate student's resilient charms," and convicts are said to "crave to twist and tear with their talons" the "very testicles" of the "gentleman whose testimony clapped them in prison for life." [78]

Observing Shade house to house through windows in the evenings, Kinbote "knew that bedtime was closing in with all its terrors. . . ." [79] One can easily infer how this homosexual might picture his good, but married friend's bedtime activities. In fact, even the phrase "closing in" may well suggest another meaning, though not another evaluative intonation.

But Humbert Humbert's narrational observations are perhaps the most relentlessly, and dramatically, sexual. Humbert "sees": the shades of female bathing suits as "dream pink, frosted aqua, glans mauve, tulip red, oolala black"; Lolita's ice-cream sundae as "erected"; his unlocked little table as "raped"; hitchhikers as "vigorously, almost priapically thrusting out tense thumbs to tempt lone women or sadsack salesmen with fancy cravings"; trees as "pubescent," "phallic," "sappy tall," "panting" (near "innerspring moss"), and as shivering with "a multitude of dappled Priaps." [80] He speaks of pressing home "the nipple" of his alarm clock and mentions Lolita's "dipping her hand into the nether anatomy of a lamp table." [81]

Nabokov has written that his "initial shiver of inspiration" for *Lolita* "was somehow prompted by a newspaper story about an ape in the Jardin des Plantes who, after months of coaxing by a scientist, produced the first drawing ever charcoaled by an animal: this sketch showed the bars of the poor creature's cage." [82] Strange as this association may at first appear, Humbert can be seen as the vividly triumphant prisoner of what he wishes his nymphet were really like. And the bars of *his* cage seem uniformly phallic.

Consider also Humbert's humorous background-like perceptions of motels—which perceptions subtly serve to vivify the undescribed (but eloquently hinted at) things that went on between himself and Lolita—"things that the most jaded voyeur would have paid a small fortune to watch." [83] For instance, Humbert "sees" motor courts with their vacancy signs as "ready to accommodate," among other occupants, "the most corrupt and vigorous couples." As usual, undescription works vividly indeed:

> Ah, gentle drivers gliding through summer's black nights, what frolics, what twists of lust, you might see from your impeccable highways if Kumfy Kabins were suddenly drained of their pigments and became as transparent as boxes of glass! . . . The Park was as black as the sins it concealed . . .[84]

At another point, Humbert dilates at length on the "obvious" uses of double motel units:

> I wondered what type of foursome this arrangement was ever intended for, since only a pharisaic parody of privacy could be attained by means of the incomplete partition dividing the cabin or room into communicating love nests . . . the very possibilities that such honest promiscuity suggested (two young couples merrily swapping mates or a child shamming sleep to earwitness primal sonorities) made me bolder . . .[85]

Even the child is involved in Humbert's imagined sexual deception. The coined word *earwitness* is typical of Nabokov and, in context, typically abets the "undescription." Few readers will notice, above, that the fantasy subtly builds upon itself: by "suggesting possibilities," the (totally imagined) honest promiscuity inferentially, insidiously, becomes more real.

One wonders, in light of all this, just what Humbert envisions as taking place in "stimulating Cincinnati." [86]

Black humor often flavors the Humbert-Hermann-Kinbote type's uniquely sexual perceptions. Humbert, for example, dreams of a future with Lolita made possible by a pregnant Charlotte's being detained in the hospital by "a nice Caesarean operation and other complications." [87] Typical also is Humbert's brief but evocative reference to his first wife while describing Charlotte: "She rubbed her cheek against my temple. Valeria soon got over that." [88] *Whatever* the word *soon* evokes, it is vivid, eloquent, and unpretty.

In *Pale Fire* the young (homosexual) King attempts to find sexual harmony with Queen Disa:

> One night when he tried tiger tea, and hopes rose high, he made the mistake of begging her to comply with an expedient which she made the mistake of denouncing as unnatural and disgusting.[89]

*Whatever* the Queen's mistake inspired, it also was probably not very pleasant. After the amusing suggestiveness of "hopes rose high," the even darker humor of the first "mistake" tends to be missed. Yet the phrase "mistake of begging" can be seen to suggest either that the King then became less, or more, insistent.

This type of detail is also provided in *Lolita* by Miss Pratt, whose insights and findings seem even to surpass Humbert's in humorously unfounded intensity:

> Dolly has written a most obscene four-letter word which our Dr. Cutler tells me is low-Mexican for urinal with her lipstick on some health pamphlets which Miss Redcock, who is getting married in June, distributed among the girls. . . .[90]

The amusingly evaluative "most obscene" highlights Miss Pratt's hypocritical ignorance of "Dolly's" hyper-specialized terminology. "Lipstick" and "Redcock" support each other in several suggestive ways.

Miss Cormorant also tends, by comparison, to mitigate the madness—even while heightening the humor—of Humbert's own hypersexual perceptual process. "We want our girls," she informs him, "to communicate freely with the live world around them . . .

> We are still groping perhaps, but we grope intelligently, like a gynecologist feeling a tumor." [91]

If one but pauses to contemplate the full implications of *intelligently,* the humor thickens, and darkens, considerably. The image is strikingly similar to Kinbote's description of how Charles II, fleeing from possible execution, sensed the "fingers of fate":

> . . . he sensed them feeling for him (as those of a grim old shepherd checking his daughter's virginity) . . .[92]

*Grim* breeds black humor as does *intelligently,* above. (Consider also Charlotte's implied and imagined "checking" of Lolita's virginity, quoted in Chapter One.)

Nabokov often deceptively intensifies the sex act or a sexual climax by use of a background atmosphere of rushing, flowing water. After Humbert's furtive climax with Lolita in his lap, for example, he says: ". . . I swept up the stairs and set a deluge of steaming water roaring into the tub." [93] His need for this steaming solvent is surprisingly descriptive. When Van first attempts intercourse with Ada, we read that "impatient young passion (brimming like Van's overflowing bath while he is reworking this . . .) burst at the lip of the orchid. . . ." [94] Hermann, who apparently has no idea of his wife's relentless copulation with her cousin Ardalion, writes:

> I longed for the hot bath I would take in my beautiful home —though wryly correcting anticipation with the thought that Ardalion had probably used the tub as his kind cousin had already allowed him to do, I suspected, once or twice during my absence.[95]

As usual, Hermann's suspicions fall teasingly wide of the mark. "Allowed him to do" points up a faint suggestion of Ardalion disrobing not only for the bath. Moreover, since Lydia is first described as "plump" and "pudgy," [96] even the phrase "used the tub" can be found quite ironic, and *correcting* is thus doubly well chosen. Also ironically, Hermann soon observes Ardalion's "need for a bath" even while ignoring copious evidence that the two cousins have just copulated.[97]

One of the most vivid scenes of sexual deception in *Laughter in the Dark* is intensified by water rushing unheeded from a bathroom tap. Margot and Rex deceive Albinus by making love in Rex's hotel bedroom after she locks the door of their "connecting" bath. When it first develops that the bathroom must be shared, Albinus asks Rex if he minds, adding: "Margot is rather splashy and long about it." (Besides being ironically prophetic in its literal meaning, this entire sentence can be read as a humorous extended sexual metaphor.)

The water then "pours in noisily." Typically, Albinus makes a feeble little joke precisely while the big joke is descending upon him: " 'You needn't lock yourself in, I'm not going to turn you out,' he called out laughingly. . . .' " We are then informed simply that "There was a loud and steady rush of water behind the locked door." The words "steady rush" seem subtly to describe the lovers' impatience—especially in conjunction with *loud* and *locked door* and since Margot has just *hurriedly* undressed for her bath.

> The water went on rushing—and grew louder and louder . . . suddenly he noticed with a shock that a stream of water was trickling from beneath the door of the bathroom. The roar of the taps had now taken on a triumphant note.[98]

The dual implication of *triumphant* is vivid and most Nabokovian. The overall image, however, is one of warm, unrestrainedly overflowing liquid, and there are even symbolic possibilities in the phrase "trickling from beneath the door." Finally, Margot calls out to Albinus the ironical partial truth: "I went to sleep in the bath."

*Pale Fire* contains a brief but quite similar sexual passage involving a running tap. Kinbote, in the commentary, relates an incident from the Zemblan monarch's boyhood.

> The two lads were told to wash their hands. The recent thrill of adventure had been superseded already by another sort of excitement. They locked themselves up. The tap ran unheeded. Both were in a manly state and moaning like doves.[99]

The dual image of unrestrained flowing is somewhat muted by the two types of more explicit excitement, but it is there. In fact, the only tangible details attending the lads are the running tap, their hands, and a distant but sensuously suggestive comparison with doves *(warm, soft, delicate, fluttery)*.

There is an extended echo of Van's "brimming bath" climax with Ada late in the novel, when the lovers are united after a long separation:

> After feasting fiercely on her throat and nipples he was about to proceed to the next stage of demented impatience, but she stopped him, explaining that she must first of all take her morning bath. . . . But mad, obstinate Van shed his terry and followed her into the bathroom, where she strained across the low tub to turn on both taps, and then bent over to insert the bronze chained plug; it got sucked in by itself, however, while he steadied her lovely lyre and next moment was at the suede-soft root, was gripped, was deep between the familiar, incomparable, crimson-lined lips.[100]

The phrase "it got sucked in by itself," especially as the reader's eye moves forward, clearly has more than one possible application. (Note also that a semicolon separates *it* from *plug* and that *plug* and *insert* both subtly prepare the reader for what follows.)

She caught at the twin cock crosses, thus involuntarily in-
creasing the sympathetic volume of the water's noise, and
Van emitted a long groan of deliverance . . . and Lucette
pushed the door open with a perfunctory knuckle knock
and stopped, mesmerized by the sight of Van's hairy rear
and the dreadful scar all along his left side.[101]

*Volume* doubly intensifies: the climax seems paralleled both by
the water's increased noise and by the "involuntary increase"
in palpable liquid flow.[102] Van's scar is the result of a duel. As
described, the "sight that mesmerizes" is surely not quite all
the reader sees; his imagination—perversely, typically—is forced
to fill in a good bit more.

Not long after, Van sits with Lucette in a music-filled res-
taurant, and she confesses drunkenness but professes a deceptively
articulate love for him:

"I'm drunk, and all that, but I adore . . . adore more than
life you, you . . . your heart was almost ripped out, my poor
*dushen'ka* ('darling,' more than 'darling'), it looked to me at
least eight inches long—"
    "Seven and a half," murmured modest Van, whose hear-
ing the music had impaired.
    "—but because you are Van, all Van, and nothing but
Van, skin and scar, the only truth of our only life, of *my*
accursed life, Van, Van, Van." [103]

*It,* as in the bathtub scene, is a dual reference—here, both to
skin and scar. And, 70 pages later (as Lucette makes a last heroic
effort to have Van before drowning herself), the two of them
speak apparently of swimming and she says: "Come with me,
hm?" He declines, but pays her a "compliment" as she returns
"to his side": "You're a divine diver. *I* go in with a messy plop." [104]
The potential sexual synecdoche becomes considerably more
vivid if one considers that "messy plop" is both echoed and
explained in "the sympathetic volume of the water's noise," above.

Early in Part Two of *Lolita* Humbert remarks:

> My lawyer has suggested I give a clear, frank account of the itinerary we followed, and I suppose I have reached here a point where I cannot avoid that chore. Roughly, during that mad year (August 1947 to August 1948), our route began with a series of wiggles and whorls in New England, then meandered south, up and down, east and west; dipped deep into *ce qu'on appelle* Dixieland, avoided Florida because the Farlows were there, veered west, zigzagged through corn belts and cotton belts (this is not *too* clear I am afraid, Clarence, but I did not keep any notes, and have at my disposal only an atrociously crippled tour book in three volumes, almost a symbol of my torn and tattered past, in which to check these recollections); crossed and recrossed the Rockies, straggled through southern deserts where we wintered; reached the Pacific, turned north through the pale lilac fluff of flowering shrubs along forest roads; almost reached the Canadian border; and proceeded east, across good lands and bad lands, back to agriculture on a grand scale, avoiding, despite little Lo's strident remonstrations, little Lo's birthplace, in a corn, coal and hog producing area; and finally returned to the fold of the East, petering out in the college town of Beardsley.[105]

"A beautiful woman should be like a compass rose of ivory . . ." Kinbote quotes a Zemblan saying characteristic of Nabokov's tendency to refer to the female body in geographic terms.[106] But first note the opening deception: Humbert implies *(chore)* that what he says will be dull; the reader is subtly advised to increase his pace. Remembering Humbert's interest in stimulating Cincinnati, the careful reader may sense something sexual in his phrase "dipped deep into *ce qu'on appelle* Dixieland." (As Proffer has noted, Humbert elsewhere puns sexually on the word *dick*.[107]) One may then possibly connect the phrase "meandered south, up and down" with Humbert's "southbound mouth" (which "briefly paused" on Annabel's "lovely indrawn abdomen" [108]). Thus, "cotton belts" may well be quite vulgar; note Humbert's fear that this may not be *"too* clear"—by now, it should be clear that his supposedly "clear, frank account of the itinerary we followed" is perhaps exceptionally "frank" but "clear" only to the very careful reader.

Upon even closer scrutiny, if we consider the total, partially retrospective context of Lolita's sexual "eye" that is so often punned upon (apparently even in "the three states beginning with 'I' " [109]), the word *itinerary,* above, now seems somewhat suggestive. "Corn belts" may even inter-echo with Lolita's "private jokes . . . transposing for instance the first letters of her teachers' names." [110] (There is a Miss Horn and a Miss Cole; note also the pun "private.") In this sense, the symmetry of "corn belts and cotton belts" exactly parallels the symmetry of Jane Austen's presumably unwitting pun in "rears and vices" that interested Nabokov. Notice also that italics tend to avert one's eyes both from the *belts* and from *Dixieland.*

The three volumes (which Humbert even offers as "almost symbolic"), considering his "pathetic Picador endearments," may also be quite ambiguous. Similarly, "southern deserts where we wintered" and "good lands and bad lands" may both be subtly suggestive.

Humbert speaks of "the undergrowth of dark decaying forests" on Charlotte's body.[111] He later mentions Lolita herself as "the faint violet whiff and dead leaf echo . . . an echo on the brink of a russet ravine, with a far wood under a white sky . . ." [112] which seems to echo "the pale lilac fluff of flowering shrubs along forest roads" here. Even "Lo's birthplace" can be read as a sexual pun, and a darkly disturbing one since (1) she is to die in childbirth and (2) they "avoid" it "despite" her "strident remonstrations." Finally, *fold* can be seen as fleshy, and the combination "petering out" can be read as a double sexual pun.

Most of Nabokov's sexual background effects are more erotically evocative and more obvious than *Dixieland.* He surely intended the following passage—a close translation of the original version composed in 1934—to be a vividly symbolic background. Cincinnatus *(Invitation to a Beheading)* speaks of interrupting his wife's unfaithfulness:

Your and his kisses, which most resembled some sort of feeding . . . when you, with eyes closed tight, devoured a spurting peach and then . . . your chin trembled, all covered with drops of the cloudy juice, which trickled down onto your bared bosom, while the Priapus who had nourished you suddenly . . . turned his bent back to me, who had entered the room at the wrong moment.[113]

The "spurting peach" and "cloudy juice" here refer to the scene itself (or its immediate aftermath) and seem almost crudely obvious. This is especially so because the next sentence begins: " 'All kinds of fruit are good for Marthe,' you would say. . . ."

Such background symbolism is more subtle when it serves to intensify an undetected episode of unfaithfulness. Near the town of Kasbeam, Humbert observes that Lolita "craved for fresh fruits." He journeys into town and, among other activities there, buys "a bunch of bananas for my monkey." [114] Laughing at the "phallic bananas," even the reader who discerns Quilty's car ("a red hood protruded in somewhat codpiece fashion") on the next page, and therefore deduces that Lolita deceived Humbert during his stint in Kasbeam—now subtly underlined by the echo of "lipstick-Redcock" in "red hood, cod-piece"—even this reader might easily miss the ultimately crystallizing connotations of Humbert's prophetically ironic observation "craved for fresh fruits." But if one has recently read *Invitation to a Beheading*, the signal may be slightly more evident—a situation so teasingly frequent in Nabokov's uniquely and synergistically interechoing world.

Such backgrounds are often placed between sexual scenes and contain a sensual suggestiveness so subtle that many readers will miss it completely—at least, consciously. Between Martha's meetings with Franz, for example, we read:

At that instant the sun swept across the soft underbelly of the white sky, found a slit, and radiantly burst through. The small trees along the path responded immediately with all their moist droplets of light. The lawn scintillated in its turn.[115]

Martha is on the gravel path approaching her house after an "Eden-like" love session in Franz's apartment. The passage can be seen to reflect not only Martha's happiness but even to echo, however faintly, quite a few details of its birth.

Even when such a background attends a sexual episode, its mechanism, in context, may be surprisingly un-obvious. Victor ("Spring in Fialta") meets Nina in a hotel "waiting for the elevator to take her down, a key danging from her fingers." "Ferdinand has gone fencing," she tells him "conversationally" and leads him along the corridor . . .

> A chair at the door of her room supported a tray with the remains of breakfast—a honeystained knife, crumbs on the gray porcelain; but the room had already been done, and because of our sudden draft a wave of muslin embroidered with white dahlias got sucked in, with a shudder and knock, between the responsive halves of the French window, and only when the door had been locked did they let go that curtain with something like a blissful sigh; and a little later I stepped out on the diminutive cast-iron balcony to inhale a combined smell of dry maple leaves and gasoline . . .[116]

The story is dated 1938, more than thirty years before the appearance of *Ada,* yet its symbolism clearly foreshadows much of the later Nabokov. (The above translation of 1957 is quite exact; Nina's "key" did not "dangle" in the original, but "only when the door had been locked" was: "only when we had locked ourselves up."[117]) Indeed, any difference seems merely in degree of emphasis: in *Ada,* the "honeystained knife" might well have been licked a time or two; in *Lolita,* the dangling key might have had a warm wooden addendum or been smoothly inserted deep in the lock; in *Despair,* Ferdinand might have been described crossing springy rapiers with a slightly moist, very nimble, golden-haired youth; and in *King, Queen, Knave* the curtain might well have flapped and struggled in a rhythmic frenzy before its "shudder" and before the "responsive halves" of the French window released it with "something like a blissful sigh." But note even here Nabokov's faintly ironic foreshadowing: "waiting for the elevator to take her down." In his 1965 Foreword to *The Waltz Invention*, Nabokov amusingly ridicules a Freudian interpretation of "the manipulation of an elevator." [118]

Finally, numerous passages in Nabokov's works that seem to have virtually no connection with explicit or even implicit sexual scenes nonetheless seem informed by an aesthetic sexual perception. Though perhaps not intended to be noted consciously, they may still make the reader more receptive to overtly voluptuous narration. Consider the following description of Pnin, after all his teeth have been extracted:

> His tongue, a fat sleek seal, used to flop and slide so happily among the familiar rocks, checking the contours of a battered but still secure kingdom, plunging from cave to cove, climbing this jag, nuzzling that notch, finding a shred of seaweed in the same old cleft. . . .[119]

Consider also how Kinbote recalls being fascinated in his "early boyhood" by a conjurer:

> I stared . . . especially at his marvelous fluid-looking fingers which could if he chose make his spoon dissolve into a sunbeam by twiddling it . . .[120]

Though hardly as explicit as the conjurer passages in *Lolita* and *Bend Sinister,* these lines can be seen to contain faint but typical Kinbotian phallic suggestions. The "twiddled spoon" that "dissolves" may be seen to inter-echo ever so faintly with the "pencil licking" and "carrot nibbling" a few pages before, and the "fluid-looking fingers" can be found to prefigure the "index finger fun" later on.

## *Notes*

1. Morris Dickstein, "Nabokov's Folly," *The New Republic* (June 28, 1969), p. 28.

2. Sigmund Freud, *A General Introduction to Psychoanalysis*, Joan Riviere, Trans. (New York, 1953), p. 164.

3. See Vladimir Nabokov, *King, Queen, Knave* (New York, 1968), pp. 13-14, 60, 74-5, 163.

4. *Ibid.*, p. 271.

5. See *ibid.*, pp. 102, 133.

6. Freud, p. 165.

7. Humbert, for example, tries to visualize the reader "as a blond-bearded scholar with rosy lips sucking *la pomme de sa canne* as he quaffs my manuscript!" (*Lolita*, New York, 1959, p. 207.) A "heavy bright-knobbed black cane" fascinates Smurov [*The Eye* (New York, 1966), pp. 3, 12] when it "twitched slightly." Pnin walks his cane "in the European manner (up-down, up-down)" (*Pnin*, New York, 1965, p. 38). See also the implied homosexual invitation with a knobbed cane in *Mary* (New York, 1970), p. 65.

   Nabokov even describes Gogol "holding that slim ivory-knobbed cane between the delicately shaped fingers of his writing hand (as if the cane were a pen)." [*Nikolai Gogol* (New York, 1934), p. 7] And later he describes certain "Gogolian little people" as "straddling Gogol's pen like a witch riding a broomstick." (p. 84)

   More, typical "fun" centers on noses, pencils, posts, sticks, and so on.

8. Vladimir Nabokov, *Ada* (New York, 1969), pp. 105, 218.

9. Vladimir Nabokov, *Despair* (New York, 1966), p. 147.

10. Nabokov, *Ada*, p. 259.

11. This device of near redundance is highly typical of Gogol. Compare also, in *Lolita*, Humbert's darkly humorous: "I took her temperature, orally . . ." (p. 219).

12. John Barth's Burlingame is said to make revolting amorous disquisitions on asparagus spears. [*The Sot-Weed Factor* (New York, 1967), p. 655.]

13. Smurov selects "a big bouquet of lilies of the valley:

   > Cold gems dropped from their bells . . . The tightly bound stems formed a thick, rigid sausage . . .

   (*The Eye*, pp. 103-4)

14. Nabokov, *Ada*, p. 259.

15. When Axel Rex feigns homosexuality to allay Albinus' presumably developing jealousy, the latter replies: "Well, that's only a matter of taste, I suppose." [Vladimir Nabokov, *Laughter in the Dark* (New York), 1961, p. 92.] (Albinus is then said to pride himself on his "broad-mindedness," a rather ironic potential pun wherein the two *broads* are faintly mutually exclusive.)

16. Having quoted Pushkin as referring to "Onegin's Journay" as "a playful parody," Nabokov comments that

   > Since the *Journey* has nothing "playful" about it (except, perhaps, the bits about the plump oysters and the traffic conditions in Odessa) and, moreover, bears no resemblance whatso-

ever to the Childe's pilgrimage, we may assume that the reference to lighthearted parody was meant to divert the censor's attention from a too-close probing of the complete text.

(*Eugene Onegin*, Vol. III, pp. 257-8)

This is of course what Nabokov himself did in *Lolita*, where the glare of pedophilia and near incest tends to outshine the many little sexual puns and salacious insinuations.

In *The Sot-Weed Factor* a raped "wench" is said to have been "near split like an oyster." (p. 334)

17. Nabokov, *Eugene Onegin*, Vol. I, p. 343.
18. Nabokov, *King, Queen, Knave*, p. 166.
19. V. Sirin (Nabokov), *Podvig* (Paris, 1932), p. 62.
20. Nabokov, *Eugene Onegin*, Vol. III, p. 298.
21. Vladimir Nabokov, *The Defense* (New York, 1964), p. 167; Vladimir Nabokov, *Zashchita Luzhina* (Paris, 1930), p. 177.
22. Vladimir Nabokov, "The Art of Fiction," *The Paris Review*, No. 41, p. 97.
23. Nabokov, *Ada*, p. 78.
24. *Ibid.*, p. 94.
25. *Ibid.*, p. 94.
26. *Ibid.*, p. 95.
27. *Ibid.*, p. 95.
28. Ada "much later" refers to the incident as "a time when the chastest of chances allowed" Van "to *snatch*, as they say, a first shy kiss!" (*Ibid.*, p. 95; my italics) Note the irony of "shy."
29. *Ibid.*, p. 55.
30. Vladimir Nabokov, *Invitation to a Beheading* (New York, 1965), p. 206.
31. *Ibid.*, p. 203. Note the "muff" pun.
32. Vladimir Nabokov, *Pale Fire* (New York, 1966), p. 30. In *Speak, Memory* [(New York, 1966), p. 306] Nabokov recalls noticing a little girl in a Paris park with a struggling Red Admirable tied to a thread: ". . . there was some vaguely repulsive symbolism about her sullen sport."
33. Nabokov, *Ada*, p. 436. In *Lolita*, Quilty tells Humbert:

> "I have been called the American Maeterlinck. Maeterlinck-Schmetterling, says I."

(p. 275; Schmetterling is "butterfly" in German)

Adducing somewhat different reasons than those obviously implied by the present reference, Alfred Appel, Jr., quotes Nabokov as saying: "That's the most important phrase in the chapter." [*The Annotated Lolita* (New York, 1970), p. 435.]

34. Nabokov, *Ada*, p. 437. My italics.
35. *Ibid.*, p. 100.
36. John Barth also vividly develops "the sexual candle":

> She lays hands upon the candle of the Carnal Mass, and mirabile,

> the more she trims it, the greater doth it wax! . . . *zut!* she caps
> his candle with the snuffer priests must shun, that so far from
> putting out the fire, only fuels it to a greater heat and brilliance.

(*The Sot-Weed Factor*, p. 360.)

Note the ingenious ambiguity of *wax*. Note also the Nabokov-like
assonance (*snuffer, must shun*) that subtly promotes an evocative tension between sound and meaning.

37. Nabokov, *Ada*, p. 53.
38. *Ibid.*, pp. 72-3.
39. *Ibid.*, pp. 116-7.
40. *Ibid.*, p. 121. My italics.
41. *Ibid.*, p. 500.
42. Vladimir Nabokov, *Bend Sinister* (London, 1960), pp. 71-2. My italics.
43. All, *ibid.*, p. 171.
44. *Ibid.*, p. 172.
45. Nabokov, *Ada*, p. 200.
46. Nabokov, *Lolita*, p. 58.
47. *Ibid.*, p. 146.
48. See *King, Queen, Knave*, pp. 28, 42, 63, 103.
49. Nabokov, *Pale Fire*, p. 128.
50. *Ibid.*, p. 28.
51. *Ibid.*, p. 117.
52. *Ibid.*, p. 167. The note typically includes another, *unexplained* Rus-
    sian pun, *Lazurchik*. *Lazurnyj* ("sky-blue") is not mentioned, although
    Kinbote does explain *siniy* ("blue").
53. Nabokov, *Ada*, p. 259.
54. Nabokov, *Pale Fire*, p. 116.
55. *Ibid.*, pp. 167-8.
56. *Ibid.*, p. 205.
57. Much of the fun in *Pale Fire* derives from seeing the truth that
    Kinbote's lies reveal—from seeing what, as Mary McCarthy has
    phrased it, "irresistibly peeps out." ["A bolt from the Blue," *The New
    Republic* (June 4, 1962), p. 21.] Indeed, Kinbote seems often to be
    least believable when he most insists. Consider his finding it "not
    worth noticing" Gerald Emerald (p. 15), his "glorious friendship" (p.
    73), and his omniscient observation about Shade:

> And perhaps, let me add in all modesty, he intended to ask my
> advice after reading his poem to me as I know he planned to do.

(p. 9)

But a careful reading of the Commentary reveals that Shade himself
was quite averse to Kinbote's even seeing the poem (which feeling the
latter so deftly misconstrues as, exclusively, pressure from Shade's wife,
p. 63). Not only is the work continually hidden from Kinbote; he must
resort, later, to bribing Shade with forbidden liquor even to hold it
in his hands. (pp. 203-4)

Kinbote vengefully terms Shade's work " 'my' poem!" (p. 130), expresses an almost morbid aversion to "help" in editing it (pp. 10, 11) and fastidiously insists upon his own pure and faithful presentation of the original (pp. 7, 11), epitomized by: "Oh yes, the final text of the poem is entirely his [Shade's]." (p. 59) Kinbote, perhaps, doth protest a bit too much. With a similar intonation, the constant cuckold Hermann claims: "Yes, she loved me, loved me faithfully." [Vladimir Nabokov, *Despair* (New York, 1966), p. 39.]

In fact, despite all imperious pretentions to impeccable scholarship, Kinbote does admit to having considered altering the text:

> It is the *only* time in the course of the writing of these difficult comments, that I have tarried, in my distress and disappointment, on the brink of falsification.

> (p. 162)

A mere two pages later Kinbote clearly admits, by implication, to having "tarried on the brink of falsification" at least once more:

> This variant is so prodigious that only scholarly discipline and a scrupulous regard for the truth prevented me from inserting it here, and deleting four lines elsewhere (for example, the weak lines 627-630) so as to preserve the length of the poem.

> (p. 164)

He thus exposes himself even by specific example.

Finally, Kinbote claims he can imitate "any prose in the world (but singularly enough not verse—I am a miserable rhymester)." (p. 204) But he obviously loves manipulating words, and his own prose passages ("suicide," p. 158; "Boscobel," p. 165) not infrequently evince a nearly cloying plenitude of poetic prose. Surely then, he *could* have altered Shade's poem, and Kinbote even goes so far as to anticipate Mrs. Shade's possible denial of the authenticity of "one or two of the precious variants." (p. 210) But the question is further complicated by the faint but leering possibility that even Shade exists only in Kinbote's imagination.

58. *Ibid.*, p. 179.
59. *Ibid.*, p. 42.
60. Freud, p. 165.
61. Nabokov, *Ada*, p. 402.
62. Nabokov, *Invitation to a Beheading*, p. 185.
63. Nabokov, *Bend Sinister*, p. 178.
64. Nabokov, *Lolita*, pp. 139, 219, respectively. As Eric Partridge remarks, having noted Shakespeare's bawdy usage of the word *rose* as *pudend; maidenhead*, "The rose with its velvet, fleshy leaves recurs in modern slang, in a slightly different sense. . . ." (*Shakespeare's Bawdy*, New York, 1969, p. 176)
65. Nabokov, *Pnin*, p. 181. Besides the obvious *rose,* there are sexual suggestions that interplay between *jewels* and *eyes.*
66. Felix, for example, wants to be someone's gardener:

. . . and then afterwards his garden would become mine, and I'd always remember my dead comrade with grateful tears. We'd fiddle together, or, say, he'd play the flute and I the mandolin.

(*Despair*, p. 85)

Pavel Mansurov sheds "tears from a certain lower orifice, no doubt" in Nabokov's translation of one of Pushkin's letters. (*Eugene Onegin*, Vol. II, p. 77) Besides other more obvious touches, such as *mine, dead, grateful, fiddle,* and *play the flute, mandolin* can also be seen to play on the fact that *dolina* in Russian means "valley."

67. Nabokov, *Pale Fire*, p. 205.
68. A former "male nurse," the man was "hard up" (supposedly, financially, p. 205) when Kinbote met him, and he is termed "versatile" when he gives Kinbote a "much-needed rubdown." (p. 114) "I hugely enjoyed," writes Kinbote,

> the aesthetic pleasure of watching him buoyantly struggle with earth and turf or delicately manipulate bulbs. . . .

> (p. 206)

The Nabokovian combination *"buoy*antly" and *"man*ipulate" helps to clarify the symbolic bulbs.
Amphibole makes for similar humor:

> How I longed to have him (my gardener, not my landlord) wear a great big turban, and shalwars, and an ankle bracelet.

> (p. 206)

But note that, with typical Nabokovian irony, the amphibole derives almost entirely from Kinbote's pausing to dispel it.
69. *Ibid.*, p. 49. My italics.
70. *Ibid.*, p. 30.
71. *Ibid.*, p. 30.
72. Typical, Hermann's phrases include "my epic calm," "a man of my stamp," and "I calmly sailed past" (*Despair*, pp. 163, 169, 170, respectively).
73. *Ibid.*, pp. 38, 42, 76, 146, 144, 192, 207, respectively.
74. *Ibid.*, p. 27.
75. Nabokov, *Pale Fire*, pp. 116, 126, 157, respectively.
76. *Ibid.*, p. 168.
77. *Ibid.*, p. 176.
78. *Ibid.*, pp. 210, 108, respectively.
79. *Ibid.*, p. 15.
80. Nabokov, *Lolita*, pp. 99, 106, 89, 146, 145, 143, 59, 154, 217, respectively.
81. *Ibid.*, pp. 244, 161, respectively.
82. *Ibid.*, pp. 282-3.
83. *Ibid.*, p. 165.
84. *Ibid.*, p. 108.
85. *Ibid.*, p. 133.

86. *Ibid.*, p. 125.
87. *Ibid.*, p. 76.
88. *Ibid.*, p. 87.
89. Nabokov, *Pale Fire*, p. 148.
90. Nabokov, *Lolita*, p. 180.
91. *Ibid.*, p. 162.
92. Nabokov, *Pale Fire*, pp. 165-6.
93. Nabokov, *Lolita*, p. 58.
94. Nabokov, *Ada*, p. 121.
95. Nabokov, *Despair*, p. 108.
96. *Ibid.*, p. 36.
97. See *ibid.*, pp. 114-6.
98. Nabokov, *Laughter in the Dark*, pp. 112-3.

    Incidentally, the "compassionate" rainy background in *Speak, Memory* (including a "bubbling" drain pipe, pp. 233-4; 238) strikingly resembles an analogous rainy night in *Mary* (pp. 67-8), and both are prefigured by fan-shaped and subtly female sunsets (*Speak, Memory*, p. 213, with a pun on "tomorrow" and *Mary*, p. 47.).

99. Nabokov, *Pale Fire*, p. 92.
100. Nabokov, *Ada*, p. 392.
101. *Ibid.*, pp. 392-3.
102. In *King, Queen, Knave* a similar "palpable liquid flow" tends (atypically) to create an "un-sympathetic" repulsiveness when Martha says: "Undress quick and hop into my bed. I have a great need." The description that follows (at Martha's apparently oblivious expense) allows for a most disillusioning meaning of *need*.

    > She left the door ajar. Her pleated skirt and jumper were already lying on a chair. From the toilet across the corridor came the steady thick rapid sound of his sister making water.

    > (p. 158)

    Perhaps the word *thick* works the greatest mischief, creating, in juxtaposition with *sound*, a deftly audio-visual repulsiveness. The use of Franz's absent sister further drains Martha's preparation of intrigue and perhaps even reminds us that she is Franz's aunt by marriage. And, since they are now in Dreyer's bedroom, Franz seems quite logically "unable to undress, let alone make love."

    Franz is obviously not an "undinist." (See *The Annotated Lolita*, Alfred Appel, Jr., ed., pp. 414-5.)

103. Nabokov, *Ada*, p. 411.
104. *Ibid.*, p. 480.
105. Nabokov, *Lolita*, p. 141.
106. Nabokov, *Pale Fire*, p. 147. Lucette employs similar directional symmetry while describing Ada's naked body (during their homosexual romps "when boyless and boiling"):

    > "... . she was . . . touched with fraise in four places, a symmetrical queen of hearts."

    > (*Ada*, p. 374)

107. Carl R. Proffer, *Keys To Lolita* (Bloomington, Indiana, 1968), p. 99.
108. Nabokov, *Lolita*, p. 39.
109. *Ibid.*, p. 192.
110. *Ibid.*, p. 178.
111. *Ibid.*, p. 72.
112. *Ibid.*, p. 253.
113. Nabokov, *Invitation to a Beheading*, p. 141.
114. Nabokov, *Lolita*, p. 194.
115. Nabokov, *King, Queen, Knave*, p. 100.
116. *Nabokov's Dozen* (New York, 1958), pp. 14-15.
117. Vladimir Nabokov, *Vesna v Fial'te i drugie rasskazy* (New York, 1956), p. 18.
118. Vladimir Nabokov, *The Waltz Invention* (New York, 1966), p. iii.
119. Nabokov, *Pnin*, p. 38.
120. Nabokov, *Pale Fire*, p. 18.

# 8.

Flaubert contrives Emma's affairs with the help of horseback riding and piano lessons. John Barth (whose style has striking affinities with Nabokov's) [1] similarly utilizes horseback riding in *End of the Road;* Nabokov has Lolita deceive Humbert during supposed piano lessons.[2] Both riding and piano playing can, of course, suggest the sex act itself. But Nabokov has developed the device still further. Martha (*King, Queen, Knave*) deceives Dreyer while allegedly participating in "oriental gymnastics," which unreal activity humorously contributes vividness to her triumphant affair with Franz. The homosexual Kinbote is forever attempting to interest others in certain special Zemblan wrestling holds. As Lucette describes her homosexual activities with Ada, the connection becomes even more obvious:

> "We interweaved like serpents and sobbed like pumas. We were Mongolian tumblers. . . ." [3]

Here, suggestive euphemism gives way to sexual metaphor, but the descriptive mechanism, including the pun on *tumble* remains the same. Far more subtly, Nabokov makes extensive cryptographic and often ingeniously evocative use of various other sports and games.

In *Lolita* sports assume a subtly symbolic sexual significance. When Humbert arrives at Lolita's summer camp to claim his filial prey, he very casually mentions noticing a report of her "behavior for July ('fair to good; keen on swimming and boating') . . ." [4] Then, during her first night with Humbert, Lolita mumbles in "sleep talk" about Barbara [5] and boating.[6] (Actually, she calls Humbert "Barbara," which Nabokov humorously exploits: "Barbara, wearing my pajamas which were much too tight for her . . ." [7])

Since Humbert has just admitted that he suspects Lolita of "some juvenile erotic experience, no doubt homosexual, at that accursed camp of hers," [8] the alert reader is thus subtly (Barbara and the boating are sleep-mentioned two pages apart) urged to discern that Lolita was perhaps "keen" on a chance to sneak away with Barbara. This, typically, is so near and yet so far. As Lolita soon explains, it was another girl, "her tent-mate of the previous summer, at another camp," who "instructed her in various *man*ipulations." [9]

Then the true reason for Lolita's "keen" interest in swimming and boating appears: copulating with Charlie, which she and Barbara regularly did while supposedly boating during July.[10]

With Quilty a playwright (author of *The Strange Mushroom* and "many plays for children" [11]), acting was doubtless destined to become a humorous euphemism for the sex act. Even his apparently very innocent "Hobbies: fast cars, photography, pets" [12] acquire additional meanings as the novel progresses.

In the wake of the "fancy embraces" presumably effected by "the magic and might" of Lolita's "soft mouth," Humbert not unproudly mentions having

> brought prices down drastically by having her earn the hard and nauseous way permission to participate in the school's theatrical program. . . .[13]

In Nabokov's works, pride almost inevitably precedes disaster.

Here, the suggestiveness of *nauseous* is subtly intensified by the potential connotations of *hard*.

Humbert soon casually remarks that Lolita and her friend Mona got "enthusiastic about dramatics" during the spring term.[14] (The careful reader may suspect this is an echo of "keen on swimming and boating.") When Miss Pratt advocates Lolita's participation in "natural recreations," Humbert jauntily asks: "Do you mean sex play?" ". . . not technically sex play," she answers, "though girls do meet boys . . ."

> "All right," I said, . . . "She can take part in that play. Provided male parts are taken by female parts." [15]

The play on *play* serves to obscure, for the casual reader, the much more complex, sustained ambiguity of the entire last sentence. And Humbert's jaunty little joke is replete with Nabokovian prophetic irony. This is further developed when Humbert has Lolita earn "permission to participate in the school play" by presumably manipulating him in her classroom behind another girl's "very naked, porcelain-white neck and wonderful platinum hair." [16] The permission to "act" is thus purchased in surprisingly similar currency. Further ironic fun includes Humbert's "perceiving" that "Lolita was irrevocably stage-struck" [17] and that perhaps "theatricals" had made her "so adorably *keen* to explore rich reality." [18]

Most important, the "playlet" in which Lolita acts is called *The Enchanted Hunters*.[19] On the surface, this merely echoes the hotel where Lolita and Humbert first made love, and further spices the sport of "enchanted hunting." Then, almost caught in her Flaubertian deception (of skipping piano lessons), Lolita claims she was unable "to resist the enchantment" of rehearsing a scene from the play with Mona. The word *enchantment* thus becomes quite vividly suggestive both of Lolita's early play with Humbert and her subsequent sprees with Quilty. Later, Humbert stresses that

> . . . she had been so pretty in the weaving of those delicate

spells, in the dreamy performance of her enchantments and duties! [20]

He then mentions the "pleasure" that Lolita's dancing gave him.

But all that was nothing, absolutely nothing, to the indescribable itch of rapture that her tennis produced in me. . . .[21]

Thus Lolita's "tennis" is introduced, by implication, as a supreme "enchantment."

Nabokov himself has termed "Lolita playing tennis" one of "the nerves of the novel," one of its "secret points" that "will be skimmed over or not noticed, or never even reached." [22] These claims and potential clues seem to justify tracing the theme of Lolita's tennis.

An early manifestation is vague, but playfully suggestive: Humbert remarks that Lolita preferred "ball hunting" to "actual play." [23] (The possible puns here, however, seem only slightly more likely in the context of "enchanted hunting.") He then mentions the "sticky closeness" of afternoon siestas with Lolita on his naked lap—

as indifferent to my ecstasy as if it were something she had sat upon, a shoe, a doll, the handle of a tennis raquet, and was too indolent to remove.[24]

The effect may seem somewhat contrived, but is still extremely subtle. The word *it* (which can seem to introduce a situation: "as if it had happened that she had sat on something . . .") more probably refers directly to *ecstasy*, which, as a humorous euphemism for Humbert's member, is vividly brought out by the raquet handle. And note the use of *remove* (rather than *move*), which tends to raise the subtle question: remove from beneath her, or from within her? Finally, although a handle is surely not normally "indolent," the culminating phrase gives rise to a teasing near ambiguity that could be significant. Were this not Nabokov, it would seem totally far-fetched to sugegst that *indolent* may have contextual shades of (too) "in Dolly" (to remove), especially since *dolina* means "valley" in Russian.[25]

Humbert later devotes more than five consecutive pages to describing the way Lolita played tennis. The sustained potential *double entendre* is very subtle, and its "secret points"—if indeed they do exist!—surely are, as Nabokov claims, easily "never even reached."

The pertinent narration includes numerous evanescently suggestive mentions of strokes, balls, control, clinging contact, and so on. At one point, Humbert wishes he had taken movies of "all her strokes, all her enchantments." [26]

> Despite her small stature, she covered . . . her half of the court with wonderful ease, once she had entered into the rhythm of a rally and as long as she could direct that rhythm. . . .[27]

Given all this, it seems possible to construe "a rally" as a single sex act. The sentence above continues: ". . . but any abrupt attack, or sudden change of tactics on her adversary's part, left her helpless." The suddenly vivid possibilities of (sexual) "tactics" nearly obscure the potential pun, "on her adversary's part."

Winning—to develop the analogy still further—can be construed as attaining a climax. Lolita, Humbert informs us, "had none of the inhibitions that cautious winners have." [28]

> So sterile were her grace and whipper that she could not even *win from panting me and my old-fashioned lifting drive.*[29]

Humbert even mentions that Lolita "melted into *winsome merriment,* my golden pet." [30]

The "tennis" description includes, typically, some rather gross potential colloquial puns. Besides insisting that "had not something within her been broken by me—not that I realized it then!—she would have had on the top of her perfect form the will to win," [31] Humbert asserts:

> Her form was, indeed, an absolutely perfect imitation of absolutely top-notch tennis—without any utilitarian results.[32]

*Form* is of course quite humorous in a sexually athletic sense. "Utilitarian results" can even be seen to suggest, within the total metaphor, becoming pregnant. And the potential pun *top-notch* has an even cruder possible echo two pages later as Humbert, discussing the rhythmical coordination of Lolita's game, adds: "—crack players will understand what I mean." [33]

Despite the frequency of such sustained potential symbolism, its "beauty" must ultimately rest in the fact that none of it—however suggestive—can ever be irrefutably demonstrated.

When Martha *(King, Queen, Knave)* watches her lover Franz play tennis, Nabokov seems to have some similar fun:

> Franz lunged and whirled but his main stroke remained a swing in a void.[34]

The sexual potential of this statement is subtly prefigured earlier. While teaching Franz to dance, Martha "gave her excitement its head, and her rapid cries expressed fierce satisfaction with his obedient piston slide." [35] Soon she tells him: "Faster, darling, much faster—don't you hear the rhythm?" and the reader abruptly learns that "They were no longer coupling on the couch, but fox-trotting" in a café. Franz's stream of consciousness then includes:

> If only he could glide thus forever, an eternal piston rod in a vacuum of delight, and never, never part from her.[36]

Almost unmistakably, the tennis phrase "swing in a void" echoes the "rod in a vacuum" here. "Rod" can refer to Franz totally or sexually, just as Martha's giving "her excitement its head," above, can be read two ways. Even the phrase "never part from her" can be construed ambiguously, as can be the "parts" in Lolita's play rehearsals.

Wtih what seems very fitting symmetry, Dreyer goes off "skiing" to deceive Martha much as she supposedly attends regular sessions of "oriental gymnastics" when he is home. Typically, Nabokov has Martha unwittingly suggest the "ski" trip by sarcastically asking Dreyer why he does not "sample" Isolda or, perhaps Ida and Isolda "both together." [37] This hint of prophetic irony is soon realized. Away to "ski," Dreyer stands at a hotel window in his pajamas with Isolda and Ida "giggling in the bathroom; but enough was enough." [38] At this point he decides to return home, "leaving his girl friends to their own devices, which were not negligible." *Devices* (as a potential pun) intensifies the implication of lesbianism (which of course also combines with the notion of sexual relations *à trois* in *Ada*).

Home, Dreyer jokes "in his best English: 'I half returned from shee-ing.' " [39] In *Ada,* Lucette expresses a fondness for "sheeing," [40] and Van employs the phrase ". . . *pendant que je shee in Aspenis.*" [41]

Just as Martha unwittingly suggests Dreyer's ski trip, she later becomes "infuriated" at the accumulation of "junk" in his desk drawers, while "shrewdly" ignoring possible photographic evidence of her husband's unfaithfulness.[42] Similarly, and almost symmetrically, Dreyer "shrewdly" notices Franz's undershorts, even joking to himself that "whoever sewed on that monogram was not a professional—at least not a professional seamstress." [43] The un-professional, of course, is his own wife.

Perhaps the most extended ironic deception of this sort involves Martha's "Oriental gymnastics" classes. Typically, Dreyer smiles at the thought that Martha too had her

. . . eccentricities. The iced rose water applied to her face at bed time. Those Hindukitsch gymnastics nearly every day.[44]

Almost predictably, Dreyer is later treated to frequent "meaning-

less" babblings about oriental gymnastics during Martha's mori-
bund delirium.[45]

The sport of swimming (in addition to its precarious symmetry to the drowning theme) suggests homosexuality in *King,
Queen, Knave*. A Mr. Schwimmer (Franz's "colleague" in selling
at the sports department)

> . . . casually informed Franz about the prizes he had won
> in swimming competitions, and Franz envied him, being
> himself an excellent swimmer.[46]

> Only once did he accompany Mr. Schwimmer to the public
> pool. The water proved to be much too cool and far from
> clean, and his colleague's roommate, a sunlamp-tanned young
> Swede, had embarrassing *manners*.[47]

Groaning, perhaps, at the pun "Schwimmer," the careless reader
tends to miss the subtle, yet surprisingly graphic humor of "only
once" and the abruptly altered false ring of "casually" (which in
retrospect seems to conceal a good deal more than boasting).
*Roommate* and even "far from clean" similarly tend to expand
in connotation.

More than a hundred pages later, it is casually dropped that
Schwimmer's "effeminate Swedish friend . . . now sold bathing
suits," [48] and still later, Dreyer snidely remarks, supposedly only
in regard to an auto-mannequin, "Scandinavian type . . . Female
impersonator, rather." [49] Finally, the sexual atmosphere about
swimming suggestively interacts with the passage comparing
Franz's love making to pearl diving.[50]

Swimming also suggests homosexual overtures in *Pale Fire*.
In fact, Kinbote meets his "gifted gardener" on the rebound, as
it were, from "a maddening and embarrassing experience at the
college indoor swimming pool." [51] The first main indications of
Kinbote's specialized sexual bent occur about midway through
his Foreword. The first of these tends to slip by in the guise of
a gross colloquial pun. Kinbote is speaking of his vegetarianism
to some colleagues at Wordsmith College during lunch:

Consuming something that had been handled by a fellow creature was, I explained to the rubicund convives, as repulsive to me as eating any creature, and that would include —lowering my voice—the pulpous pony-tailed girl student who served us and licked her pencil.[52]

Very typically, the blatantly Freudian pencil-licking tends to detract from the potential pun "eating." This pun's orientation, though by no means exclusively homosexual at first, is soon clarified by a series of ever more revealing suggestions.

Kinbote proceeds to refer, casually, to his colleagues as "grinning old males." He also mentions "a moody, delicate, rather wonderful boy." And then, he informs us that a "tormentor"

inquired if it was true that I had installed two ping-pong tables in my basement. I asked, was it a crime?" No, he said, but why two? "Is *that* a crime?" I countered, and they all laughed.[53]

The implications are still vague. A page later, however, Kinbote hurries off "to have a kind of little seminar at home followed by some table tennis, with two charming identical twins and another boy, another boy." [54] Here, the duality of youths and repetition of phrasing serve subtly to multiply Kinbote's boys almost beyond the capacity of two pingpong tables. And the word *crime*—also recently repeated—tends to re-echo strangely and vividly by virtue of its original association with table tennis. The faint pun on *charming* similarly tends to echo *wonderful*, above, and the phrase "a kind of little seminar" seems rather revealing in its neatly verbose vagueness.

Thus it now seems almost certain that the "old males" were "grinning" and a good deal more *at*, than *with*, our madman, which he dauntlessly misinterprets: "My free and simple demeanor set everybody at ease." [55] It is from precisely this kind of inspired distortion that the main ironic humor of *Pale Fire* derives.

Kinbote subsequently introduces a sport considerably more

appropriate than ping-pong for veiling homosexual advances. Rather casually, he mentions "a treatise on certain Zemblan calisthenics in which I proposed to interest that young roomer of mine. . . ." [56]

> A week later he was to betray my trust by taking sordid advantage of my absence on a trip to Washington whence I returned to find he had been entertaining a fiery-haired whore from Exton who had left her combings and reek in all three bathrooms. Naturally, we separated at once. . . . I can forgive everything save treason.[57]

Strategic detail evokes "crime," investigation, and even emotional reaction, so that Kinbote's roomer seems irrevocably unworthy of Zemblan calisthenics. *Naturally* can be read "by nature" (in addition to "it goes without saying"), both *trust* and *treason* seem susceptible to homosexual construction.

Later there is evidence to suggest that the hiring of Kinbote's "gifted gardener" helped to compensate for this "treason" as well as for the swimming pool mishap.[58] Kinbote also tells of "a very enjoyable and successful meeting of students and teachers (at which I had exuberantly thrown off my coat and shown several willing pupils a few of the amusing holds employed by Zemblan wrestlers) . . ." [59] Though *willing* may reflect a humorous misunderstanding on Kinbote's part, the ambiguous *successful* seems both vivid and far-reaching in its implications.

As in the phrase "manly and moaning like doves," [60] homosexual activities elsewhere in *Pale Fire* are amusingly termed "manly." Fleur for example "did not seem to mind" when the Prince "abandoned her for manlier pleasures . . ." [61] When Queen Disa "found out all about our manly Zemblan customs," she "concealed her naïve distress . . ." [62] The young King apparently tried to reform, "but everywhere along the road powerful temptations stood at attention." (Note the sustained ambiguity of these last three words.) As further described, the "temptations" include acrobats and bareback riders, whose suggestive potential fits in quite vividly with the general theme of manly calisthenics.

At another point, Kinbote claims to be "a tricky wrestler" and "an enthusiastic rock-climber." [63] He also mentions "lithe youths diving into the swimming pool of a fairy tale sport club." [64] Soon after, he even uses the word *games* as an apparent euphemism for masturbation.[65]

After the Zemblan revolution, Kinbote reveals that through Odon "the King kept in touch with numerous adherents, young nobles, artists, college athletes, gamblers, Black Rose Paladins, members of fencing clubs, and other men of fashion and adventure." [66] Among many "sporting" possibilities, the words *in touch* and *members* seem especially suggestive. "Members of fencing clubs," in fact, can be seen to conjure up amusing homosexual connotations indeed.

In Nabokov's short story "Spring in Fialta" Ferdinand is cuckolded while he "has gone fencing." [67] Later he appears sucking a long stick of candy, while

> Beside him walked the dapper, doll-like Segur, a lover of art and a perfect fool; I never could discover for what purpose Ferdinand needed him. . . .[68]

If this "need" is sexual, the deceiver is typically deceived.

In a state of shock from discovering Lolita's piano lesson deception, Humbert exposes his chess queen in a game with the homosexual Gaston. Suspecting a possible trap, Gaston

> . . . shot furtive glances at me, and made hesitating half thrusts with his pudgily bunched fingers—dying to take that juicy queen and not daring—and all of a sudden he swooped down upon it (who knows if it did not teach him certain later audacities? . . .[69]

The chess queen symbol seems appropriate in both size and shape because Gaston favors young boys. *Juicy* functions as an ingenious pun, especially since Humbert constantly reads so much sex into his surroundings.

In *Speak, Memory* more than five consecutive pages (ostensibly devoted to "the composing of chess problems") contain a sustained potential sexual analogy.[70] Besides phrases such as "how to mate," "the building hand gropes for a pawn in the box," "blind throbbings," "the quality of my relief," "a dual solution," and so on, there is mention of "the old Russian end-game studies, which attain the sparkling summits of the art." (This can be seen to have some humorous chauvinistic echoes.[71])

Soviet problems are then rather snidely said to replace "artistic strategy by the ponderous working of themes to their utmost capacity.

> Themes in chess, it may be explained, are such devices as *forelaying, withdrawing, pinning, unpinning* and so forth; but it is only when they are combined in a certain way that a problem is *satisfying*." [72]

After mentioning how, in concocting problems, he was "always ready" to cause "form to bulge and burst like a sponge-bag containing a small furious devil," Nabokov explains some particulars:

> This or that knight is a lever adjusted and tried, and readjusted and tried again, till the problem is tuned up to the necessary level of beauty and surprise.[73]

The passage seems to have sensual overtones even if we do not take *knight* as a pun. Nabokov also employs, however, the casual but potentially signal phrase (discussed at length in Appendix D, below, as tipping off "those in the know"): "this or that."

Among suggestive phrases, Nabokov describes the "mellow physical satisfaction" of composing chess problems:

> There is a feeling of snugness . . . play-planing in bed . . . there is the nice way one piece is ambushed behind another, within the comfort and warmth of an out-of-the-way square; and there is the smooth motion of a well-oiled and polished machine that runs sweetly at the touch of two forked fingers lightly lifting and lightly lowering a piece.[74]

Though far from explicit, the potential sexual analogies here seem scarcely in need of explication. One should remember however that woven into context, such phrases seem almost totally unsuspicious. And, obviously, nothing can be proved.

With striking similarity to the "moth-firefly" passage in *Bend Sinister,* this chess problem digression culminates in a statement by Nabokov that "the information concealed in my chess symbols . . . may be, and in fact is, divulged." Ostensibly these words refer to one of his favorite old problems, but (like the "conjurer's set" in *Bend Sinister*) they can also be found to hint, not un-ironically, at other possibilities as well.

Chatting with Shade, Kinbote mentions "the preposterous game of nature" and observes that there may be no "rules." [75] "There are rules in chess problems: interdiction of dual solutions, for instance" is Shade's somewhat disconnected reply. But taken sexually, the phrase "dual solutions" seems a rather appropriate interdiction for a homosexual who speaks of nature as a game without rules.

Reading a Soviet chess magazine, Fyodor (*The Gift*) finds "a charming four-mover" that includes a "cleverly hidden mating device" and "a hermetic stalemate." [76]

M'sieur Pierre (*Invitation to a Beheading*) carries on a two-page monologue while playing chess with Cincinnatus.[77] Although he seems almost to alternate erotic observations with statements about the game, there are few, if any, interplays of meaning. Pierre does call Cincinnatus' wife "a juicy little piece," however, and he twice uses the word *piece* with reference to chess.

Krug (*Bend Sinister*) recalls the schoolyard of his childhood:

> The yawn of the tunnel and the door of the school, at the opposite ends of the yard, became football goals much in the same fashion as the commonplace organ of one species of animal is dramatically modified by a new function in another.[78]

Whether in reference to animal or organ, the combination "in another" succeeds as a rather dramatic sexual pun. Consider also *commonplace.*

The above passage seems further developed by means of sensual detail two pages later.

> . . . because the goal was a door.
>     If you opened the door you found a few *zaft*-pupen ["softies"] mooning on the broad window seats behind the clothes racks, and Paduk would be there, too, eating something sweet and sticky given him by the janitor, a bemedaled veteran with a venerable beard and lewd eyes. When the bell rang, Paduk would wait for the bustle of flushed begrimed classbound boys to subside, whereupon he would quietly make his way up the stairs, his agglutinate palm caressing the banisters.[79]

Given the "school-door (sexual) goal" metaphor, the ringing of the bell which touches off a finally subsiding rush of classbound boys seems an ingenious extension of the figure. And if we wonder why the janitor "with lewd eyes" was so generous to Paduk "behind the clothes racks," the boy's "agglutinate palm caressing the banisters" becomes quite suggestive.

In *Laughter in the Dark*, Rex tries to persuade Margot against the background of a hockey game to slip off and sleep with him. Their conversation is interrupted by the news that a goal-keeper "slid slowly toward his tiny goal," [80] "the goal-keeper pressed his legs together," [81] and "the noise had reached its climax: a goal had been scored . . ." [82] Not long after, when Rex arrives at Albinus's house and meets Paul (whose presence at the hockey game had frightened Albinus away): "They looked at one another and—there was a great outburst of cheering as the puck was shot into the Swedish goal." [83] This echo, which obviously suggests recognition, seems also sexually prophetic: Paul and Albinus soon leave, and Margot and Rex make love.[84]

Ada and Van are constantly hampered in their earlier amorous exploits by the presence of Lucette. On one occasion, this little playmate's rubber doll gets swept away by the current of a brook.

> Van shed his pants under a willow and retrieved the fugitive. Ada, after considering the situation for a moment, shut her

book and said to Lucette, whom usually it was not hard to enchant, that she, Ada, felt she was quickly turning into a dragon, that the scales had begun to turn green, that now she *was* a dragon and that Lucette must be tied to a tree with the skipping rope so that Van might save her just in time. For some reason, Lucette balked at the notion but physical strength prevailed. Van and Ada left the angry captive firmly attached to a willow trunk, and, "prancing" to feign swift escape and pursuit, disappeared for a few precious minutes in the dark grove of conifers. Writhing Lucette had somehow torn off one of the red knobbed grips of the rope and seemed to have almost disentangled herself when dragon and knight, prancing, returned.[85]

The next day, for similar purposes, Ada insists that Lucette have a long, soaking bath:

"I'm Van," said Lucette, standing in the tub with the mulberry soap between her legs and protruding her shiny tummy.[86]

Eight pages later, we read that

By the way, she had confessed, Ada had *made* her confess, that it was, as Van had suspected, the other way round—that when they returned to the damsel in distress, she was in all haste, not freeing herself, but actually trying to tie herself up again after breaking loose and spying on them through the larches. "Good Lord," said Van, "that explains the angle of the soap!"[87]

The syllogism is thus complete: Lucette may get loose and see all; she definitely did not; she definitely did.

After a slow and humorously vague awakening ("after considering the situation for a moment"), the plan takes rapid, almost breathless shape. In fact, the very pace of its realization seems reflected in purposely jerky narration that finally flows free and fast, and the description of Ada's becoming a dragon thereby seems subtly to suggest the companion image of Lucette's resistance to counter the lovers' overeager advances.

Also typical is the pleasure conveyed by the word *prancing* —first, pleasant anticipation; second, sexual satisfaction plus smugness at having deceived. Such glee fares ill in Nabokov's scheme of Fate.

In retrospect, we can surmise that Lucette—despite the whiff of suspicion about her forced confession—probably tore off one of the gripes while fully freeing herself. In context, cunning juxtaposition creates the illusion that the tearing was done while attempting unsuccessfully to escape. And note the carefully worded phrase *"seemed to have* almost disentangled herself (rather than *"had* almost . . ."). Our deception, in this respect, was fastidiously "honest." And the returning lovers' impression thus insidiously presumes to be omniscient narration, yet this is actually far from so. Moreover, the phrase "save her just in time," in retrospect only, becomes justified with rather biting prophetic irony. (Lucette was indeed saved "just in time"—any sooner, and she presumably could not have fooled her "deceivers.")

Finally, this little incident seems surprisingly vital to the total structure of *Ada*. Lucette's rubber doll is a playfully obvious echo of Aqua's "surprised little fetus, a fish of rubber she had produced in her bath, in a *lieu de naissance* plainly marked X in her dreams." [88] The following sentence (which introduces Van's rescue of the doll) thus seems to develop the disturbing echo still further: "With the sudden impatience of inanimate things, the doll managed to get swept away by the current." [89] Moreover, the sentence immediately preceding the description of Aqua's fetus contains what seems to be a further preview of the "prancing" scene: ". . . panic and pain, like a pair of children ing a boisterous game, emitted one last shriek of laughter and ran away to manipulate each other behind a bush. . . ." [90] (Note the Nabokovian combination of *bois*terous and *man*ipulate.)

But the doll also functions most effectively as a prophetic symbol. For Lucette, decisively spurned in her passion for Van, is later to drown herself. Prior to this, she surprises Van and Ada in the act of sexual intercourse, and thus the entire dragon game, as well as the loss of the doll, becomes ingeniously prophetic.

# *Notes*

1. Besides the oyster, candle, *A*, and asparagus parallels mentioned elsewhere in this study, general similarities range from love of parody, black humor, deception (such as fictitious forewords and syllogistic narrational twists) and irony (even including a parallel ironic use of adverbs such as *pleasantly* and *cheerfully*, prevalent in *End of the Road* and *Laughter in the Dark*) to a fondness for wordplay, proverb-play, and even initials, monograms, and the prefixes *a-* and *be-*.
2. Vladimir Nabokov, *Lolita* (New York, 1959), p. 185.
3. Vladimir Nabokov, *Ada* (New York, 1969), p. 375.
4. Nabokov, *Lolita*, p. 103.
5. *Ibid.*, p. 118.
6. *Ibid.*, p. 120.
7. *Ibid.*, p. 118.
8. *Ibid.*, p. 114.
9. *Ibid.*, p. 125. My italics. Such partial puns with *man* seem especially effective in descriptions of lesbian activities, but obviously such nomenclitorial play can be overemphasized.
10. *Ibid.*, p. 126.
11. *Ibid.*, pp. 31-2. Mushrooms and toadstools are often quite obviously phallic in Nabokov's works. See, for example, *Ada*, pp. 119, 405 and *Despair* (New York, 1966), p. 65. Alfred Appel, Jr. quotes Nabokov as relating, in this connection: "Somewhere, in a collection of 'cases,' I found a little girl who referred to her uncle's organ as 'his mushroom.'" [*The Annotated Lolita*, Alfred Appel, Jr., ed (New York, 1970), p. 349.]
12. Nabokov, *Lolita*, p. 32.
13. *Ibid.*, p. 168.
14. *Ibid.*, p. 174.
15. *Ibid.*, p. 179.
16. *Ibid.*, pp. 180-1.
17. *Ibid.*, p. 182.
18. *Ibid.*, p. 190. My italics.
19. *Ibid.*, p. 183.
20. *Ibid.*, p. 210.
21. *Ibid.*, p. 210.
22. *Ibid.*, p. 287.
23. *Ibid.*, p. 149.
24. *Ibid.*, p. 151.
25. There are numerous vaguely suggestive usages of *mandolin* in Nabokov's novels, especially *Despair*. Note also Kinbote's joke regarding Sybil Shade's "mandolin tights" [*Pale Fire* (New York, 1966), p. 62] and—if one accepts the theory outlined above that Kinbote could have altered "Pale Fire"—line 640 of the poem: "Pale jellies and a floating

mandolin." (*Ibid.*, p. 40) The end of the preceding line ("A medium smuggled in") can even be seen to refer, cryptographically, to Kinbote.

26. Nabokov, *Lolita*, p. 212.
27. *Ibid.*, p. 212.
28. *Ibid.*, p. 212.
29. *Ibid.*, p. 213. My italics.
30. *Ibid.*, p. 214. My italics.
31. *Ibid.*, p. 212.
32. *Ibid.*, p. 211.
33. *Ibid.*, p. 213. At one point Humbert says he got Lolita to take tennis lessons from "a famous coach . . . with a harem of ball boys. . . ." (*Ibid.*, p. 148) "Given the context," Alfred Appel, Jr., suggests, "the prosaic phrase and vocation of 'ball boy' becomes a pun." (*The Annotated Lolita,* p. 386. See also "this or that," p. 148).
34. Vladimir Nabokov, *King, Queen, Knave* (New York, 1968), p. 188.
35. *Ibid.*, p. 151.
36. *Ibid.*, p. 152.
37. *Ibid.*, p. 147.
38. *Ibid.*, p. 154.
39. *Ibid.*, p. 160.
40. Nabokov, *Ada*, p. 464.
41. *Ibid.*, p. 466.
42. Nabokov, *King, Queen, Knave*, p. 184.
43. *Ibid.*, p. 186.
44. *Ibid.*, p. 205.
45. *Ibid.*, p. 256.
46. *Ibid.*, p. 78.
47. *Ibid.*, p. 80. My italics.
48. *Ibid.*, p. 203.
49. *Ibid.*, p. 263.
50. *Ibid.*, p. 166.
51. Nabokov, *Pale Fire*, p. 205.
52. *Ibid.*, p. 13.
53. *Ibid.*, p. 13.
54. *Ibid.*, p. 14.
55. *Ibid.*, p. 13.
56. *Ibid.*, p. 17.
57. *Ibid.*, p. 17.
58. See *ibid.*, p. 155.
59. *Ibid.*, p. 71.
60. *Ibid.*, p. 92.
61. *Ibid.*, p. 79.
62. *Ibid.*, pp. 148-9.
63. *Ibid.*, p. 85.
64. *Ibid.*, p. 86.
65. *Ibid.*, p. 90.
66. *Ibid.*, p. 87.
67. *Nabokov's Dozen* (New York, 1958), pp. 14-15.
68. *Ibid.*, p. 18.

69. Nabokov, *Lolita*, p. 185.
70. Vladimir Nabokov, *Speak, Memory* (New York, 1966), pp. 288-93.
71. Consider, above, "the acrobatic brilliance of the Russian rhyme." Compare also:

> As is usual in Russian, the not-on-foot character of coming is specified.

> [Vladimir Nabokov, *Eugene Onegin* (New York, 1964), Vol. III, p. 20]

72. Nabokov, *Speak, Memory*, p. 289. My italics.
73. *Ibid.*, p. 290.
74. *Ibid.*, p. 291.
75. Nabokov, *Pale Fire*, p. 161.
76. Vladimir Nabokov, *The Gift* (New York, 1963), p. 198.
77. Vladimir Nabokov, *Invitation to a Beheading* (New York, 1965), pp. 144-5.
78. Vladimir Nabokov, *Bend Sinister* (London, 1960), p. 58.
79. *Ibid.*, p. 60. Nabokov's brackets.
80. Vladimir Nabokov, *Laughter in the Dark* (New York, 1961), p. 83.
81. *Ibid.*, p. 83.
82. *Ibid.*, p. 84.
83. *Ibid.*, p. 93.
84. *Ibid.*, p. 97.
85. Nabokov, *Ada*, p. 143.
86. *Ibid.*, p. 144.
87. *Ibid.*, p. 152.
88. *Ibid.*, p. 25.
89. *Ibid.*, p. 143.
90. *Ibid.*, p. 25.

# Conclusion

Having capsulized the plot of *Laughter in the Dark* in four short lines, Nabokov proceeds: "This is the whole of the story and we might have left it at that had there not been profit and pleasure in the telling." [1]

Nabokov's haunting magic rests precisely in the telling—in his particular combination of sounds, words, ideas. The result is an achievement allegedly denied Cincinnatus in *Invitation to a Beheading*: a pleasing interaction enabling

> . . . a commonplace word to come alive and to share its neighbor's sheen, heat, shadow, while reflecting itself in its neighbor and renewing the neighboring word in the process, so that the line is live iridescence. . .[2]

The mechanisms, as explored in the present study, are both subtle and complex. For Nabokov's world breathes with a teasing and unseen deception. Describing himself as a Russian writer, he has aptly emphasized "the mirror-like angles of his clear but weirdly misleading sentences." [3]

A faintly Russian coloration further contributes to the "live iridescence" of Nabokov's English prose. His writings evince a unique perspective on especially these two languages and cultures.

But Nabokov's uniquely controlled "reality" is surely his

most mysterious product. Elusive inter-echoes, from line to line, from book to book, subtly expand. Systematic networks of ironic foreshadowings produce a background unsettling in its depth. Hidden levels of meaning effect a striking range of dimension.

Nabokovian "reality" also illustrates his belief that imagination is a form of memory. His narrators (for example, Humbert, Hermann, Kinbote) view and present their stories through the lenses of their own imaginations. Memory and imagination systematically overlap. And the clear, vivid results of their purposely blurred interaction consistently make up for a negation of time.

Sex moreover permeates all: even the dullest and most unlikely objects are frequently enlivened by a sexual vibrancy. In fact, a strangely insistent sexual perception of reality imparts a live iridescence to Nabokov's entire world. Sexual self-dramatization is the alembic; the distillation, a blending of bright idealization and shadowy humor. This sexual essence, ironically enough, is no doubt easily missed by many readers of *Ada* and *Lolita*. For nothing on the surface of Nabokov's world is totally to be trusted. He writes from a grandly isolated pinnacle; the full impact of his masterful details is not for the casual reader. But these details, when savored, give rise to a curiously alien, yet almost bewilderingly unified whole. "Looking at it objectively," Nabokov has declared, "I have never seen a more lucid, more lonely, better balanced mad mind than mine." [4]

## Notes

1. Vladimir Nabokov, *Laughter in the Dark* (New York, 1961), p. 5.
2. Vladimir Nabokov, *Invitation to a Beheading* (New York, 1965), p. 93.
3. Vladimir Nabokov, *Speak, Memory* (New York, 1966), p. 288.
4. *Time*, May 23, 1969, p. 82.

> The nature of literary genius has always attracted speculation, and it was, as early as the Greeks, conceived of as related to "madness" (to be glossed as the range from neuroticism to psychosis).

> [René Wellek and Austin Warren, *Theory of Literature* (New York, 1956), p. 69.]

# Appendix A.

## The Negative Comparison

First it may be useful, by way of definition, to show what the negative comparison might be like if it existed in English. Colloquially, the combinaton "It's not a bird; it's not a plane; it *is* superman" seems most appropriate. In a more poetic, but also rather alien vein, consider the line "My love is not a red, red rose" as working naturally to establish a final image of rose-like beauty.

The negative comparison, it should be clear, is quite unnatural to English. If the device does occur at all, it seems almost experimental, as in the popular song:

> It's not the pale moon that excites me,
> That thrills and delights me,
> Oh, no—it's just the nearness of you.

Shakespeare can be seen to employ a negative construction resembling the negative comparison:

> When sorrows come, they come not single spies,
> But in battalions.

Notice however that the "sorrows" seem more convincing in English when first affirmed. Melville similarly approaches the Russian patterning with:

> Such dreary streets! blocks of blackness, not houses, on either hand . . .[1]

In Russian, a negative comparison might well read: ". . . not blocks of blackness, houses . . ."

One may also find scattered examples in English of descriptive forces similar to those that function in the negative comparison. The resulting effect, however, is almost invariably humorous.

> Well, after that, of course, everything was simple. . . . Mervyn returned with a cardboard box . . . and about four hours later was mounting the front-door steps of Clarice Mallaby's house in Eaton Square with the box tucked under his arm.
>
> No, that is wrong. The box was not actually tucked under his arm, because he had left it in the train. Except for that, he had carried the thing through without a hitch.[2]

> Then Mr. Inflammable Gass ran and shov'd his head into the fire and set his hair all in a flame, and ran about the room—No, no, he did not; I was only making a fool of you.[3]

Here, the device may be deemed little more than playful negation, but notice how the denied images almost unseriously linger. It is this effect that Nabokov has systematically capitalized upon in his English prose, as illustrated in the chapter above.

Curiously little has been written about the negative comparison. Critics seem either to take the figure for granted [4] or to content themselves with a terse definition:

> . . . its first part is descriptive—consists of an image that is presented with negation. The bard seems to be warning us

that further discourse will not be about what he is saying now, but about something else.[5]

Vladimir Weidlé has helpfully implied that the device is best explained as a psychological phenomenon: Once a descriptive image appears, the very fact of its selection tends suggestively to outweigh its negation.[6]

In English however, negation can easily render selection ironic. For instance (in answer to "How strong is he?") one says "Well, he's no Hercules," the implication is presumably that the man is rather weak. But in Russian, irony is generally caustic, un-humorous; and the form "He's no Hercules, but he's very strong" would seem more probable. This basic linguistic contrast may be seen in the following comparison. Potebnya writes that "total negation is impossible." He explains negation in language as "a collision of positive magnitudes."

> . . . if someone says: "This paper *is not white,* we may presume that the first impression forced him to reproduce a previous idea of paper's whiteness, while the succeeding impression forced this idea out of his consciousness . . . the predicate was unable to withstand the force of the succeeding impression, which will be expressed in words if we say: "This is not white, but grey paper." [7]

Indeed, the reader hardly expected the paper to be red, or black. The word "white" was presumably selected—especially in Russian—for its closeness, and the paper, one feels, may even be quite a light grey.

Writing about the English language, William Empson has suggested:

> . . . in searching for greater accuracy one might say "2 per cent white" and mean a very black shade of grey.[8]

The two approaches seem to reveal signal opposing descriptive tendencies. In Russian, description enjoys both positive and negative access to its object, whereas in English the positive approach seems greatly preferred.

Incidentally, one of the longest negative comparisons in Russian literature is double in structure and consists of no less than 28 lines (the ending of A. K. Tolstoy's poem "Ioann Domaskin").

Finally, Nabokov's affinity with Gogol is reflected in their employment of negative-comparison-like forces. Andrey Bely (in his article "Gogol' ") uses similar constructions 27 times—4 times quoting Gogol and 23 more while describing Gogol's style.[9]

## Notes

1. Herman Melville, *Moby Dick* (New York, 1962), p. 27.
2. P. G. Wodehouse, *Mulliner Nights* (New York, 1933), pp. 125-6.
3. William Blake, *The Poetry and Prose of William Blake* (New York, 1965), p. 443.
4. See L. I. Timofeev, *Osnovy teorii literatury* (Moscow, 1963), p. 205.
5. B. V. Tomashevskij, *Stilistika i stikhoslozhenie* (Leningrad, 1959), p. 211.
6. V. Vejdle, "O smysle stikhov," *The New Review*, Number 77, p. 134.
7. A. Potebnya, *Mysl' i yazyk* (Kharkov, 1913), p. 180.
8. William Empson, *Seven Types of Ambiguity* (New York, 1955), p. 217.
9. Andrej Belyj, *Lug zelënyj* (New York, 1967), pp. 96-119.

# *Appendix B.*

*A Selection of Passages
Wherein Sound
Instrumentation, Especially
Assonance, Contributes
to Meaning
in Nabokov's Works*

*Bend Sinister* (London, 1960):

> . . . the man must be a very Satan of persuasiveness . . .
> (p. 42)

*Invitation to a Beheading* (New York, 1965):

> . . . like a man unable to resist arguing with a hallucination,
> even though he knows perfectly well that the entire masquer-
> ade is staged in his own brain . . . (p. 213)

[My italics]

"An Affair of Honor" (*Nabokov's Quartet,* New York, 1966):

. . . a half squashed chocolate eclair on a plate released its creamy inside . . . (p. 14)

[By virtue of assonance, the releasing seems more creamy, and the creamy seems more released.]

From the street he saw that the bedroom windows of his flat were aglow, conveying the soothing news that his wife was at home. (p. 15)

["Soothing news" forms a bridge of both sound and meaning between "aglow" and "home."]

*The Waltz Invention* (New York, 1966):

(*The phone rings hopelessly*).

[This is a stage direction.]

*Speak, Memory* (New York, 1966):

I try again to recall the name of Colette's dog—and, tri-umphantly, along those remote beaches, over the glossy eve-ning sands of the past, where each footprint slowly fills up with sunset water, here it comes, here it comes, echoing and vibrating: Floss, Floss, Floss! (pp. 151-2)

["Floss" of course does "echo" with "glossy." More subtly, the similar "aw" sound in "recall" and in "Colette's dog" can be seen to simulate phonetically the described attempt to remember "Floss."]

*Pale Fire* (New York, 1966):

Oh, switch it off! And as life snapped we saw
A pinhead light dwindle and die in black
Infinity. (p. 35)

We all know those dreams in which something Stygian soaks through and Lethe leaks in the dreary terms of defective plumbing. (p. 164)

[Notice how "soaks through" prepares the reader for "Lethe leaks."]

"Spring in Fialta" *(Nabokov's Dozen,* New York, 1958):

. . . the old, slate-blue sidewalk, which ret*ai*ned here and there a f*a*ding memory of *a*ncient mos*a*ic design. (p. 7)

[My italics. Note also the secondary assonance common to both "sidewalk" and "design."]

*Laughter in the Dark* (New York, 1961):

He took *li*fe *li*ghtly, and the only human feeling that he ever experienced was his keen *li*king for Margot . . . (p. 101)

[My italics. Here, the secondary assonance is offered by "feeling" and "keen."]

*Pnin* (New York, 1965):

. . . an awful suspicion crossed his mind. (p. 19)

. . . a bridle path felted with fallen leaves . . . (p. 23)

*The Defense* (New York, 1964):

Playing with his cane and snapping the fingers of his free hand, he went out into the corridor and began to walk at random, ending up in a courtyard and thence making his way to the street. (p. 247)

[Here, the meaning-enhancing assonance seems arranged in pairs of words: playing, cane; snapping, hand; began, random; making, way. Alliteration also contributes: fingers, free.]

*The Gift* (New York, 1963):

. . . the crimson mist of shame. (p. 52)

. . . that touch of dismal idiocy which is inherent in any war . . . (p. 147)

. . . pangs of disgusting jealousy which he strove not to probe . . . (pp. 208-9)

[Note the evocative tension effected by assonance in "strove" and "probe."]

. . . with everlastingly creased pants . . . (p. 214)

. . . gnomelike lamps, miserably posing as vessels of doziness, glowed on six or seven little tables . . . (p. 230)

. . . the russety fuzz which looked as if stuck onto his cheeks . . . (p. 247)

# Appendix C.

*A Selection of Additional
Passages in Nabokov
Promoting the Reader's
Creative Participation
by Tincturing the "Unreal"
with the "Real"*

*Despair* (New York, 1966):

. . . the little puff of smoke that slowly stretched out in midair, was folded by ghostly fingers, and melted away. (p. 65)

. . . the above-mentioned adolescent does not, in the morning, deign to glance at the photograph he had adored in bed. (p. 108)

*Pnin* (New York, 1965):

. . . he lay on his sickbed, wiggling his toes and shifting phantom gears. (p. 113)

"Cloud, Castle, Lake" *(Nabokov's Dozen,* New York, 1958):

. . . Vasili Ivanovich became so exhausted that during the midday halt he fell asleep at once, and awoke only when they began to slap at imaginary horseflies on him. (p. 87)

*Bend Sinister* (London, 1960):

. . . a cold breeze lifted with invisible finger and thumb the silvery mane of the old mare. (p. 94)

*Pale Fire* (New York, 1966):

I was an infant when my parents died.
. . . I've tried
So often to evoke them that today
I have a thousand parents. (p. 25)

. . . insofar as he was capable of imagining a palpable future . . . (p. 197)

*The Defense* (New York, 1964):

. . . a long, long interval of thought, during which Luzhin bred from one spot on the board and lost a dozen illusionary games in succession . . . (p. 136)

*Ada* (New York, 1969):

. . . a gigantic footman (not existing in the house but killable in the dream . . . (p. 97)

. . . consulting a calendar he did not see. (p. 370)

*King, Queen, Knave* (New York, 1968):

Dreyer briefly cast up his eyes to a makeshift heaven and made no reply. (p. 7)

The sun penetrated her eyelids with solid scarlet, across which luminous stripes moved in succession (the ghostly negative of a passing forest) . . . (p. 9)

[Martha on the train]

*Speak, Memory* (New York, 1966):

I can visualize her, by proxy, as she stands in the middle of the station platform, where she has just alighted, and vainly my ghostly envoy offers her an arm she cannot see. (p. 98)

. . . I discovered one day in the New York Public Library, indexed under my father's name, a copy of the neat catalogue he had had privately printed when the phantom books listed therein still stood, ruddy and sleek, on his shelves. (p. 182)

At times, some additional rustle, troubling the rhythm of the rain in the leaves, would cause Tamara to turn her head in the direction of an imagined footfall . . . (pp. 233-4)

"Mademoiselle O" *(Nabokov's Dozen)*:

Somehow those two sleighs have slipped away; they have left my imaginary double behind on the blue-white road. (p. 131)

[In *Speak, Memory* "my imaginary double" is rendered as "a passportless spy" (p. 99).]

*Laughter in the Dark* (New York, 1961):

As he waited for her at the door, his mind went out to track her. Now she would have entered the hotel; now she would be coming up in the lift. He listened for the click of her heels along the corridor. But his imagination had out stripped her. (p. 123)

[The descriptive mechanism here is not unlike "The Pursuit" device that Nabokov identifies with "the basic structure of Chapter One" of *Eugene Onegin* (Vol. II, p. 108).]

"A Forgotten Poet" *(Nabokov's Dozen)*:

One had the odd impression that presently he would lead you into the next (non-existing) room, where supper would be served. (p. 38)

[Notice how the serving of supper helps to solidify the non-existing room, much as "ruddy and sleek, on his shelves" helps to bring out the "phantom books," above, in *Speak, Memory*.]

"The Assistant Producer" *(Nabokov's Dozen)*:

Ghostly multitudes of ghostly Cossacks on ghost-horseback are seen charging through the fading name of the assistant producer. (p. 55)

*Lolita* (New York, 1959):

For the benefit of old-fashioned readers who wish to follow the destinies of the "real" people beyond the "true" story . . . The caretakers of the various cemeteries involved report that no ghosts walk. (p. 6)

Once or twice I was on the point of burning the unfinished draft . . . I was stopped by the thought that the ghost of the destroyed book would haunt my files for the rest of my life. (p. 283)

The *Eugene Onegin* Commentary (New York, 1964):

*Hamlet* is finished not only because the Danish prince dies, but also because those whom his ghost might haunt have died too. (Vol. III, p. 311)

# Appendix D.

### This and/or that

Deep in *Ada* the reader is treated to a lecture by Van "on the general character of dreams."

> A writer who likens, say, the fact of imagination's weakening less rapidly than memory, to the lead of a pencil getting used up more slowly than its erasing end, is comparing two real, concrete, existing things . . . the pencil I'm holding is still conveniently long though it has served me a lot, but its rubber cap is practically erased by the very action it has been performing too many times.[1]

Here of course the stereotyped Freudian pencil finds metaphorical extension into a humorous sexual analogy. Two of the more obvious possibilities are "served" and "rubber cap." The idea that this rubber cap "erases" what the pencil's lead "creates" seems quite ingenious. "Too many times" suggests vaguely amusing regret in both contexts of meaning. Less obviously, "the fact of imagination's weakening" and "memory" can be seen to hint at a need for sustaining mental images during the act. Van continues:

> Similiarly, when a teashop humorist says that a little conical titbit with a comical cherry on top resembles *this or that* (titters in the audience) he is turning a pink cake into a

pink breast (tempestuous laughter) in a fraise-like frill or frilled phrase (silence).[2]


As so often happens in Nabokov, the reader who smiles at one hidden meaning may well be in blissful ignorance of one or more others. He who grins at the tit in titbit may miss its twin in titters, and vice versa. And both may miss the fact that "titters" functions as a potential pun: not only "laughter," perhaps, but "breast specialists" in the audience.[3] And the reader who espies both the two breasts and the specialists may well not realize that "titbit" echoes a passage on copulation among "flies" long before.[4] Even the word "teashop" may be phonetically read "T-shop."

But note the parenthetical laughter-pause that follows the almost too coy euphemism "this or that." Since Nabokov so often slips a relatively subtle joke by in the wake of another, more obvious one—the casual words "this or that" may well warrant further investigation.

The fact is that this shameless little phrase (slightly modified as "this and that") plays a significant role in Nabokov's *Eugene Onegin* Commentary. Too extensive to reproduce here in full,[5] this role may be summarized as follows: Pushkin, mentioning the sparkle, briskness, and froth of "Clicquot or Moët" in Chapter Four of the novel, adds: "(A simile of this and that)." Nabokov spends much of four pages suggesting most convincingly that Pushkin slyly intended to recall "to those who were in the know" an eleven-line passage in Baratinski's *Feasts,* which culminates:


> . . . it bursts its cork with sportive surf
> and merrily its foam doth spurt
> —a simile of youthful life . . .[6]


*This* symbolism, too obvious to require explication, surely surpasses the above cupcake in good, unclean fun. But most readers of *Ada,* smugly smiling, will miss the allusion entirely. Nabokov had even recently (24 pages earlier) employed the same Moët image in *Ada:* ". . . the golden globules ascending quick-quick in this flute of Moët . . ." [7]

But is there any evidence that the (above-summarized) elaborate fuss over "this and that" is really to be identified with *Ada's* "this or that," even by "those in the know"? It seems so. In an article called "The Servile Path," Nabokov has said, of "the complications attending the turning of *Eugene Onegin* into English":

> My main contention was, and is, that the translator, in order to be lucidly faithful to his text, should be aware of *this or that* authorial reminiscence. . . .[8]

In his actual Foreword to the translation, Nabokov renders what is presumably the same pertinent phrase as "should be aware of *every such* authorial reminiscence." [9] The alteration seems difficult to explain except as a little joke for "those in the know."

Echoes can be found in Nabokov's other writings. For example, after an "admirer" of Pnin's wife secretly arranges for a critic to praise her mediocre poetry,

> Pnin, *who was not in the know,* carried about a folded clipping of that shameless rave in his honest pocketbook, naively reading out passages to *this or that* amused friend . . .[10]

Soon after, we read of a "tension-releasing" psychiatric-patient group wherein *"this or that* lady" would vividly describe her husband's performance the night before "to her still blocked but rapt sisters." [11]

Of his teaching at Cornell, Nabokov has written:

> . . . I deeply enjoyed the chuckle of appreciation in *this or that* warm spot of the lecture hall at *this or that* point of my lecture. My best reward comes from those former students of mine who ten or fifteen years later write to me to say that they now understand what I wanted of them when I taught them to visualize Emma Bovary's hairdo or the arrangement of rooms in the Samsa household or the two homosexuals in *Anna Karenina.*[12]

In Nabokov's works it often seems that a few tantalizing manifestations of an apparent theme have been prepared expressly to undermine systematic analysis and to embarrass conscientious pursuit. Ostensibly referring to Shade's weakness for alcohol, Kinbote remarks:

> Well did I know he could never resist a golden drop of *this or that,* especially since he was severely rationed at home.[13]

Kinbote is inviting Shade over for the evening. Given the would-be host's homosexual bent, the "golden drop of this or that"—despite its potentially ironic tone of wishful thinking—does seem consistently reinforced, in the sexual sense, by "severely rationed at home." But this possible cryptography, if intended at all, seems intended as a teasing mirage.

Finally, see also the phrase "this or that knight" in Nabokov's very suggestive remarks about the satisfaction of composing chess problems (discussed above in Chapter Eight).

## *Notes*

1. Vladimir Nabokov, *Ada* (New York, 1969), p. 363.
2. *Ibid.,* p. 363. My italics. The "conical-comical" interplay is most Nabokovian.
3. As early as *Bend Sinister* Nabokov can be seen (especially if one recalls the scene wherein Mariette is obviously trying to arouse Krug sexually) to employ a strikingly similar pun as a one-word sentence:

    She looked down at the agony of his senses. Tittered.

    (*Bend Sinister,* London, 1960, p. 172.)

    The potential pun becomes especially ingenious if one remembers that Mariette is dressed in her nightgown, and hence, while she "tittered" (in the sense of laughing), the punnish meaning presumably became concurrently vivid.
        Late in *Laughter in the Dark,* when Rex and Margot derive a portion of their pleasure by being affectionate before the very eyes of totally blind Albinus, a chapter ends:

    Albinus fancied that someone—not Margot, but someone by the side of Margot—tittered softly.
    (*Laughter in the Dark,* New York, 1961, p. 149.)

Especially with a very literal reading of "by the side of Margot," both the last two words serve as potential puns.

4. Nabokov, *Ada,* p. 135.
5. In addition to the four pages summarized here, see Pushkin's own note (Vladimir Nabokov, *Eugene Onegin,* New York, 1964, Vol. I, p. 327) and Nabokov's note, with several other references (*Ibid.,* Vol. III, p. 298).
6. *Ibid.,* Vol. II, p. 481.
7. Nabokov, *Ada,* p. 339. This in turn seems to recall *Lolita:* ". . . those luminous globules of gonadal glow that travel up the opalescent sides of juke boxes" (*Lolita,* New York, 1959, p. 124)—which, in turn, perhaps even re-echoes in *Ada* as "a masturbating jazzband" (*Ada,* p. 484), "jazz" thus serving as a suggestive pun.
8. Vladimir Nabokov, "The Servile Path," *On Translation,* Reuben A. Brower, ed. (New York, 1966), p. 97. My italics.
9. Nabokov, *Eugene Onegin,* Vol. I, p. x. My Italics.
10. Vladimir Nabokov, *Pnin* (New York, 1965), pp. 45-6. My italics.
11. *Ibid.,* p. 51. My italics.
12. Vladimir Nabokov, "The Art of Fiction," *The Paris Review,* No. 41, pp. 108-9. My italics.
13. Vladimir Nabokov, *Pale Fire* (New York, 1966), pp. 203-4. My italics.

# *Appendix E.*

*l, v*

There is ample evidence to suggest that Nabokov's sexual symbolism includes the suggestive shapes (and perhaps even the colors!) of the letters "l" and "v." *The Real Life of Sebastian Knight* contains the following passage (from one of Sebastian's novels):

> Life with you was lovely—and when I say lovely, I mean doves and lilies, and velvet, and that soft pink 'v' in the middle and the way your tongue curved up to the long, lingering 'l.' [1]

Here Nabokov not only evokes a delicate tactile softness (doves, lilies, velvet), blending into a visual softness (soft pink)—the letters "l" and "v" surely hint at more. And, propitiously, the "female" v *is* in the middle of "lovely," and the tongue does curve up when making, phonetically, a long, lingering l.

In *Speak, Memory* Nabokov explains his "fine case of colored hearing" by ascribing precise shades, tints and hues to various letters of the alphabet. (These colors, he finds, are evoked by orally forming a given letter while imagining its outline.) Amusingly enough, one of his "whites" is "noodle-limp l." [2]

> . . . and today I have at last perfectly matched *v* with "Rose Quartz" in Maerz and Paul's Dictionary of Color. [3]

Soon after Van's first night with Ada, we watch him watching blue butterflies:

> At the present moment he was looking forward to collecting what he would recollect later, and watched the big bold Blues as he sprawled on the turf, burning with the evoked vision of Ada's pale limbs in the variegated light of the bower . . .[4]

It seems most appropriate that the butterfly (a familiar symbol) makes Van burn (also familiar) with his vision of Ada in the bower (where the butterfly symbol was established). In the next sentence we are told that later "his foreglimpse of live ivory" was quite "accurately reproduced":

> He had resolved to deal first of all with her legs which he felt he had not feted enough the previous night; to sheath them in kisses from the A of arched instep to the V of velvet . . .

Key, strategic "v's" lead directly to Ada: "evoked vision . . . variegated light . . . live ivory . . . V of velvet." The letter "l" also often recurs, especially in "collect" and "recollect" (already sexually symbolic in the context of "watching butterflies").

Ada's monogram (Ⱅ) [5] may be seen to combine not only her initials but also the letters l and v. And Van, who is so agonizingly close to both Ada and Lucette, is frequently represented by V.V.[6] There is also in *Ada* a clandestine organization (one of whose functions is to help "sexually starved potentates" deceive their wives) called VPL. The initials allegedly stand for "Very Private Letters." [7]

The *Ada* asparagus passage (discussed above, wherein the diners were described as introducing "orally" the "voluptuous ally of the prim lily of the valley") now seems quite generously reinforced by potentially symbolic "v's and "l"s. And this may now be compared with Margot (*Laughter in the Dark*):

Her love was of the lily variety; but now and then it burst into flame and at such times Albinus was deluded into thinking he had no need of any other love-mate.[8]

Lilies of the valley seem faintly sensual in *The Defense* [9] and far more obviously so in *The Eye:* "The tightly bound stems formed a thick, rigid sausage" and "cold gems dripped from their resilient bells." [10] Also in *The Eye* Smurov finds it "amusing" to envision a "modest-looking" girl's "depraved devices of love play." [11] The girl he sadly loves is called Vanya ("Johnny"), and she is described as wearing "a white pullover with a low V neck." [12]

Sebastian's reference to "velvet," above, and Ada's "V of velvet" are typical. Indeed, "velvet" is one of Nabokov's favorite words, and the "v"s therein frequently seem sexually symbolic. In his short story "The Vane Sisters" for instance we read that D. (who loved one sister, Sybil, before her suicide) "must have known" her body "down to its last velvet detail." [13] "No matter," Humbert Humbert avers, "even if . . .

> her lovely young velvety delicate delta be tainted and torn—
> even then I would go mad with tenderness . . . my Lolita." [14]

The numerous "l"s between the "v"s before "tainted and torn" seem potentially, if darkly humorously, quite suggestive.

Earlier on the same page Humbert says: "She was only the faint violet whiff and dead leaf echo of the nymphet I had rolled myself upon with such cries in the past; an echo on the brink of a russet ravine . . ." The "russet ravine" seems a most suggestive potential symbol. But note that the italicized "l"s, if read as sexually symbolic, appear with surprisingly appropriate timing.

The first night, when Humbert envisions Lolita naked and unconscious, with a "velvet" hair ribbon in her hand,[15] there is a prefiguring of the ("tainted and torn") "velvety delta" passage:

> . . . lust is never quite sure—even when the velvety victim
> is locked up in one's dungeon—that some rival devil or in-
> fluential god may still not abolish one's prepared triumph.[16]

The "l"'s in key words are also numerous here, and "influential" seems vaguely punnish. Humbert then mentions Lolita's "ivory pale legs" and on the next page he claims: "If a violin string can ache, then I was that string."

But the word "velvet" is perhaps most sensuously suggestive in *Ada*. Early in the novel D'Onsky, watching a painting, "allowed his undisguised gaze to caress the velvety apple and the nude's dimpled and mossed parts with a smile of bemused pleasure." [17] Due perhaps to similar visual caresses and descriptive juxtaposition, "mossed parts" and "velvety apple" seem almost signally in league. Van finds "ravishing" the "velvety rose" of Cordula de Prey's "cheeks" while he lives with her.[18] Violet Knox (Van's typist) has "a velvet carnation and a tweed-cupped little rump." [19] The humorously punnish velvety parallel (rose . . . cheeks; carnation . . . rump) is indeed striking. But there are many more evocative usages of "velvet" in *Ada* alone.[20]

In contrast to *Ada, Lolita* and *The Real Life of Sebastian Knight,* both *King, Queen, Knave* and *Invitation to a Beheading* were written originally in Russian, so the "l" and "v"'s of "velvet" (in their English versions) are less significant. "Velvet" in Russian is *"barkhat,"* which does however have phonetic affinities with both *Marta* (Martha) and *Marfin'ka* (Marthe). Thus, in *Invitation,* Cincinnatus' "jumbled" nocturnal stream of consciousness ("Marthe, the executioner's block, her velvet . . ." [21]) was in the Russian signally linked by assonance: *"Marfin'ka, plakha, bar-khat . . ."* [22] And when Marthe obtains permission to see Cincinnatus by means of "a little concession," and then "the tight bodice of her black velvet dress was heaving," [23] "velvet dress" *(barkhat-nogo plat'ya)* was similarly linked to *Marfin'ka* by sound in the Russian.[24]

Early in the novel Cincinnatus thinks of "that black velvet which lines at night the underside" of Marthe's "eyelids." [25]

> . . . and there was a black velvet ribbon on her soft, creamy white neck, and the velvety quiet of her dress flared at the bottom, blending with the darkness.

All this seems strikingly like Martha *(King, Queen, Knave),* whose eyes have "adorable dark lids slightly creased like violets" [26] and whose neck is termed "velvety-white" [27]—which suggestively combines with the idea of its "creamy texture and lines" as "a token of all kinds of marvels." [28] (The focus on Marthe's "velvet-on-creamy-white" subtly moves to her flaring skirt through the echo "velvety," while Martha's "velvety-creamy-white" is "tokenly" assigned below.[29])

Such mutually reinforcing, teasingly *déjà-vu*-like effects which echo from book to book are of course typical. Marthe's "rosy kisses tasting of wild strawberries" [30] for instance seem to inter-echo with Martha's "luscious lascivious strawberry yawn" [31] and perhaps even with Ada's tongue, kissing Van: "A large boiled strawberry, still very hot." [32]

In *King, Queen, Knave*, Franz (sexually aroused) imagines Martha in bed with her husband, hearing "the divine violin." [33] His next words (in this stream of consciousness as he opens a door) are "Damn this key," which can be construed as an Aesopian apology—to "those in the know"—for the V symbolism, much as Humbert's "but this must stop" humorously excuses his constant references to "locking Lolita up you know where." [34]

Generally, evocative "l"s and "v"s occur most frequently in *Ada* and *Lolita*. In *Ada* there is much ado about the Venus Villa Club (a chain of pleasure houses [35]), "the girls" of which are at one point described as needing the "absolute prerequisites," among others, of "impeccable buttocks and breasts, and the unfeigned *v*im of a*v*id *v*enery." [36] And "a tattling tabloid reported" that " 'Velvet' Veen traveled once—and only once—to the nearest floramor with his entire family." [37] There is also "naked Ivory Revery (a model)." [38] Consider also the strategic "l"s in the above-mentioned images of "golden globules" ascending a "flute" of Moët *(Ada)* and the "luminous globules of gonadal glow that travel up the sides of juke boxes" *(Lolita)*.

The pills with which Humbert tries to render Lolita susceptible to gentle violation are "Violet blue." [39] She is later described by Humbert as haunting his sleep. "Shedding shift after shift," Lolita

. . . would recline in dull invitation on some narrow board

or hard settee, with flesh ajar like the rubber valve of a soccer ball's bladder.[40]

Potentially suggestive "l"s and "v"s are numerous.

Early in the novel Humbert speaks of his "prophetic nymphet" Annabel's "lost loveliness" and their "brief session of avid caresses in the violet shadow of some red rocks forming a kind of cave." [41] Then he relates their "unsuccessful first tryst."

> One night, she managed to deceive the vicious vigilance of her family. In a nervous and slender-leaved mimosa grove at the back of their villa . . . that vibrant sky seemed as naked as she was under her light frock. . . . Her legs, her lovely live legs, were not too close together, and when my hand located what it sought, a dreamy and eerie expression, half-pleasure, half-pain, came over those childish features.[42]

Additional evocative "l"s and "v"s may be seen in two of Humbert's lustful schemes: "before such a vastness and variety of vistas" [43] and "Venus febriculosa." [44] Consider also his speciously denied scheme: ". . . never did my fancy sink its fangs into Lolita's sisters, far far away, in the coves of evoked islands." [45] "Islands" perhaps echoes Lolita's sexual "i," traced at length above. And, since Humbert employs many ingenious and humorously elegant euphemisms for his own sexual organ, "fancy" can be seen to inter-echo with the (now punnish) "fancy embrace" discussed above.

Finally, although the letters "l" and "v" are surely Nabokov's subtly suggestive favorites, there may well be others. In *Ada* for instance one reads of a Spanish "anatomical term with a 'j' hanging in the middle." [46]

## Notes

1. Vladimir Nabokov, *The Real Life of Sebastian Knight* (Norfolk, Conn., 1959), p. 112.
2. Vladimir Nabokov, *Speak, Memory* (New York, 1966), p. 34.
3. *Ibid.*, p. 35.
4. Vladimir Nabokov, *Ada* (New York, 1969), pp. 128-9.
5. *Ibid.*, p. 47.

John Barth's Burlingame remarks that "Your A . . . represents the forked crotch of man, the source of seed, and also, by's peak and by's cross-line, the union of twain into one . . ." (*The Sot-Weed Factor*, New York, 1967, p. 493.)

6. See *Ada*, pp. 56, 73, 184, 472, and especially 170.
7. *Ibid.*, p. 329.
8. Vladimir Nabokov, *Laughter in the Dark* (New York, 1961), p. 10.
9. Vladimir Nabokov, *The Defense* (New York, 1964), p. 52.
10. Vladimir Nabokov, *The Eye* (New York, 1966), pp. 103-4.
11. *Ibid.*, p. 76. My italics.
12. *Ibid.*, p. 98.
13. *Nabokov's Quartet* (New York, 1966), p. 79.
14. Vladimir Nabokov, *Lolita* (New York, 1959), p. 253.
15. *Ibid.*, p. 115.
16. *Ibid.*, p. 116.
17. Nabokov, *Ada*, p. 13.
18. *Ibid.*, p. 322.
19. *Ibid.*, p. 576.
20. See especially *ibid.*, pp. 76, 350, 418. See also pp. 9, 33, 41, 78, 103, 148, 169, 197, 203, 226, 250, 307, 472, 486.
21. Vladimir Nabokov, *Invitation to a Beheading* (New York, 1965), p. 66.
22. Vladimir Nabokov, *Priglashenie na kazn'* (Paris, 1938), p. 75.
23. Nabokov, *Invitation to a Beheading*, p. 195.
24. Nabokov, *Priglashenie na kazn'*, p. 191.
25. Nabokov, *Invitation to a Beheading*, p. 20.
26. Vladimir Nabokov, *King, Queen, Knave* (New York, 1968), p. 10.
27. *Ibid.*, p. 38.
28. *Ibid.*, p. 6.
29. In the Russian *King, Queen, Knave* Martha's "velvety-white neck" was "naked" (*goluyu*). (*Korol', dama, valet*, New York, 1968, p. 40.) The English edition however has been spiced by the phrase "her bare legs crossed"—an addition that seems further to emphasize the "token" association of V above with "marvels" below.
30. Nabokov, *Invitation to a Beheading*, p. 28.
31. Nabokov, *King, Queen, Knave*, p. 11.
32. Nabokov, *Ada*, p. 103. See also p. 437.
33. Nabokov, *King, Queen, Knave*, p. 120.
34. Nabokov, *Lolita*, p. 187, discussed in Chapter Seven above.
35. See *Ada*, pp. 176, 348-58.
36. *Ibid.*, pp. 351-2. My italics.
37. *Ibid.*, p. 350.
38. *Ibid.*, p. 36.
39. Nabokov, *Lolita*, p. 113.
40. *Ibid.*, p. 231.
41. *Ibid.*, p. 15.
42. *Ibid.*, p. 16.
43. *Ibid.*, p. 67.
44. *Ibid.*, p. 181.
45. *Ibid.*, p. 235.
46. Nabokov, *Ada*, p. 46.

# *Appendix F.*

## *Lolita's* Sexual Eye — I

Potential references to Lolita's *Eye-I* as a sexual symbol are considerably more numerous than those examined above in Chapter Six. When Lolita persuades Humbert to take another trip so that she and Quilty can continue their affair more conveniently, she asks: ". . . we'll go wherever *I* want, won't we?" (p. 189, Nabokov's italics). Humbert soon says: ". . . I once read a French detective tale where the clues were actually in italics . . ." (p. 192). Describing his conversation with Lolita about her relationships with Quilty and Dick, Humbert remarks, apparently of himself: "And *I* had never counted, of course?" (p. 248, Nabokov's italics; two pages later, Humbert himself estimates the number of times she and Dick have had intercourse).

References are often sly and tinged with black humor. Consider her "eye-strain" (p. 178) and "absolutely enchanting smile for strangers, a tender furry slitting of the eyes" (p. 260). Making secret arrangements with Quilty by telephone, she "slit her eyes at" Humbert (p. 189). Phrases like "opening her eyes and raising herself slightly" (p. 254) are typical. Consider also Humbert's generalization: "the tragic eyes of unsuccessful blondes" (p. 266). Lolita's "I.Q." (p. 139) may even connect her cryptographically with Quilty; and "Quelquepart Island" (p. 228) may even relate to "Dixieland," perhaps "By putting the geography of the *United States* into motion" (p. 139, my italics). Finally, there is Humbert's sly licking of a dull, mad speck from Lolita's "salty eyeball" and his very sly question: "Now the other?" (p. 42).